The Road to Reward

The Road to Reward

A Biblical Theology of Eternal Rewards

2nd Edition

by Robert N. Wilkin

The Road to Reward: A Biblical Theology of Eternal Rewards

Wilkin, Robert N., 1952–

ISBN: 978-0-9883472-2-9

Copyright © 2003, 2014 by Grace Evangelical Society

4851 S I-35 E, Suite 203
Corinth, TX 76210
www.faithalone.org
ges@faithalone.org
940-270-8827

Design: Shawn C. Lazar

Printed in the United States of America

To Shawn, Mark, Bethany, and Kyle
—friends and coworkers
who help me keep my eyes on the prize!

Contents

Section 1
Is Eternal Salvation a Reward?

"Now to him who works,
the wages are not counted as grace but as debt.
But to him who does not work
but believes on Him who justifies the ungodly,
his faith is accounted for righteousness."

Romans 4:4-5

CHAPTER 1

The Disaster of Poor Communication

On July 28, 1945, the heavy cruiser *Indianapolis* left Guam for Leyte Gulf, in the Philippine Islands. She radioed the standard message to Leyte that she was on her way, but due to atmospheric interference the signal was scrambled, and Leyte received nothing intelligible.

This lack of communication proved disastrous, for at 12:15 a.m. on July 29, the *Indianapolis* was hit by two torpedoes from a Japanese submarine, the first one knocking out the electrical system, preventing an SOS call. She sank in twelve minutes. Nine hundred of the 1,200 men aboard survived the sinking, taking refuge in the few lifeboats afloat or clinging to debris, hoping for a quick rescue. However, since no one knew when the ship was expected in port, the sailors waited in vain. Over three days passed before search planes finally spotted the survivors—only 316 of the original 900 were still alive. It was a tragic loss caused by poor communication.[1]

I understand the disaster of poor communication. As a young boy, I joined a religious group that taught that eternal life was something you earned—something that came to you only after a good deal of personal sacrifice and holy living. An offshoot of a Holiness church, this group was incredibly extreme in its views and convinced me that if I didn't get my life cleaned up enough, I might miss even the *opportunity* to be saved. However, they did assure me that if I succeeded in cleaning my life up before my window of

---

[1] Virgil Hurley, *Speaker's Sourcebook of New Illustrations* (Dallas, TX: Word Publishing, 2000), 91.

opportunity came (a period of one to two weeks that could occur anytime between the ages of five and twenty), then salvation was mine. Now as depressing as that was—it got worse. They also taught that once I had obtained eternal life, I would lose it if I committed *even one sin*—with no chance of ever getting it back.

My experience in that religious group influenced me in more ways than one. Early on, it made me very *resistant* to the grace of God. However, once God broke through my resistance, my background actually compelled me to become a strong *advocate* for the grace of God and the freeness of eternal life.

Now I realize that it might seem strange to start a book on eternal rewards by talking about eternal life; however, there's good reason to begin here. You see, many people in our world think just as I did—that eternal life *is* our reward. As a teenager, eternal life was something I was fervently striving to gain and keep. It *was* the eternal reward I sought. But this was only another example of the disaster of poor communication.

Eternal Life Is Free

In contrast to the message I heard as a young man, the Lord Jesus spoke of eternal life, not as a *reward*, but as "the *gift* of God" (John 4:10, emphasis mine). Jesus made a simple yet profound promise: "He who believes in Me has everlasting life" (John 6:47). We can take Him at His word. He is not trying to trick us. The Lord Jesus guarantees eternal life to all who simply believe in Him for it (compare 1 Timothy 1:16). It really is that simple! And once we believe in Him, we can begin to obey Him in the matter of laying up treasure in heaven.

Whenever justification salvation is presented as a reward, there are at least three negative side effects.

First, if we lose this distinction, we also lose assurance. We can't be sure we are born again unless we know that eternal life is a gift that is received simply by faith in Jesus Christ. Only the biblical gospel unmixed with rewards theology allows the Christian to remain sure that he has everlasting life.

Second, we cannot evangelize clearly if we fail to recognize this difference. How can we help someone else find assurance if we are not sure ourselves? If we are wondering whether we have done enough to have everlasting life, then we can't possibly share the good news clearly with others.

Third, once this distinction is abandoned, our motivation to live for Christ becomes distorted. Instead of being motivated out of love, gratitude, and a desire for reward, we are motivated by fear of hell. Legalism is the offspring of insecurity. When eternal life *is* the reward, we cease to be properly motivated to live for God.

When You Doubt

It's clear from Scripture that God doesn't want you to be in doubt about your eternal destiny. He wants you to *know* that you have eternal life (1 John 5:13). So if you lack assurance, why not ask God to show you the truth and to make His Word understandable to you?

Also, I suggest that you read the Gospel of John through several times, praying for God to open your eyes. Take the time to highlight all of the promises God makes to those who simply believe in Christ for eternal life. The promises of God are the key to finding assurance of salvation. We are not saved through the promises *we* make to God but through the promises *He* makes to us! You can rest your eternal destiny confidently on this promise from the Gospel of John. Jesus said:

> "For God so loved the world that He gave His only begotten Son, that whoever believes in Him should not perish but have everlasting life" (John 3:16).

You can take Christ at His word—*whoever* believes in Him for everlasting life has it! He has never broken a single promise He has ever made. He never will.

Conclusion

As we begin a consideration of eternal rewards, I don't want to be guilty of poor communication: *eternal life is absolutely free, but eternal rewards are not.* John 6:47 and many other passages make it clear that the only thing God requires of us for eternal life is faith in His immutable promise. This is important because, when we lose sight of this fact, all the rewards passages of the New Testament suddenly become a list of instructions for what we must do to obtain and keep eternal life. And when people view rewards passages this way, assurance is lost and along with it, the most powerful motivation for serving God found in the Bible—gratitude for His "indescribable gift" (2 Corinthians 9:15).

CHAPTER 2

Wages Aren't Gifts

University professors in England went on a one-day strike in the spring of 1999 to protest their salaries. The Association of University Teachers was seeking a ten percent pay raise and subsequently rejected an offer of a 3.5 percent increase.

In the summer of 2000, teachers in Australia sought a thirty percent pay raise. Later that year Air Afrique pilots went on a one-day strike over their salaries.

NFL referees rejected an offer in 2001 that would have given them an immediate forty percent pay increase and doubled their pay within two years.

Everyone wants to earn a fair wage—hence the rise of unions and strikes and salary negotiations. Indeed, God's Word indicates that we should receive fair wages: "The laborer is worthy of his wages" (Luke 10:7; 1 Timothy 5:18).

Wouldn't it be fantastic to know that for the rest of your life no employer would underpay you? You would receive completely fair compensation for the work you did. Sure, that would be great. We all want to get our fair share from our labors.

As important as our salaries are, they are of little significance compared to what we will receive from the Lord Jesus in eternity for serving Him in this life. There will be no need to negotiate our eternal compensation for serving Christ now. The Lord promises to give us what is fair.

We work for pay in our jobs here and now. But to many Christians the idea of working for the Lord Jesus for pay is a completely foreign concept. To them, serving Jesus is something they should do because they love Him, because it is their duty, because they want to please Him, and because they know life goes better when they live it God's way.

While all of those are admirable motivations for service, it is vital that every Christian knows that when he is serving Christ, he is working for wages.

Rewarded for Works

The Greek word translated *rewards* is *misthos*. When a day laborer worked a twelve-hour day, he was paid his wages, or *misthos*. See Matthew 20:1-16.

There are twenty-nine New Testament occurrences of *misthos*.[1] As you study these, you will see that rewards are something more than the gift of everlasting life believers receive at the moment of faith.

They are not, however, the only passages dealing with the doctrine. Many other texts allude to the concept without using the word *misthos*. Other key rewards words and phrases you will encounter are "approval" (*dokimos*), "disapproval" (*adokimos*), "ruling with Christ," "inheriting the kingdom," "reaping everlasting life," "blamelessness," "being confessed by Christ," "boldness or shame at His coming," "the Judgment Seat [Bema] of Christ," and "Jesus as Judge."

Justified by Faith

As I stated in the previous chapter, many people have the idea that entering the kingdom is a reward. They figure that if they make it, then they have all the reward that anyone could want. Yet look at Paul's words in Romans 4:4-5:

---

[1] There are ten occurrences by Matthew (5:12, 46; 6:1, 2, 5, 16; 10:41 (twice), 42; 20:8); six by Paul (Romans 4:4; 1 Corinthians 3:8, 14; 9:17, 18; 1 Timothy 5:18); four by Luke (Luke 6:23, 35; 10:7; Acts 1:18); four by John (John 4:36; 2 John 8; Revelation 11:18; 22:12); two by Peter (2 Peter 2:13, 15); and one each by Mark (9:41), James (5:4), and Jude (11).

Now to him who works, the wages [*misthos*] are not counted as grace but as debt. But to him who does not work but believes on Him who justifies the ungodly, his faith is accounted for righteousness.

Notice how the doctrine of rewards must be understood in order to maintain the doctrine of justification by faith alone. The person who thinks that he must do good works to stay justified, or to prove he is justified, does not believe that God *justifies the ungodly*. Nor does he believe that *his faith is accounted for righteousness.* Jesus guarantees eternal life to all who simply believe in Him (John 11:25-27).

We must keep the distinction between wages and grace. Otherwise we obscure assurance and the good news. And we cannot hope to accurately witness to others if we mistakenly think that justification is a reward.

Distinct and Separate

When you get your paycheck, you don't thank your employer for the gift, do you? Most likely you think, "I'm grateful to have a job I enjoy that pays me a livable wage. I earned this and I can put it to good use."

Now let's say you were in serious financial need and a person at your church simply gave you $1,000 so that you could make your mortgage payment and avoid losing your house. Would you think, "Wow, it's great that I earned this money"? No. Most likely you would say, "Thank the Lord for such a wonderful and thoughtful gift. I don't deserve it, but I really appreciate it."

Make no mistake here. Eternal life is a gift.[2] Rewards are not. We must keep these two distinct.

In this life we receive our wages once or twice a month. God pays us in this life in many ways as well—and more than once or twice a month. He gives us the fruit of the Spirit. He provides us with food to eat, clothes to wear, and a place to stay. But our ultimate payday will occur after this life is over when we as believers will appear at the Judgment Seat of Christ.

---

[2] More precisely, *the present reception of eternal life in Jesus* is a gift. There are passages (see Chapter 3, for example), in which *a potential future gaining of eternal life* is clearly a reward. There, however, mere life is not in view. Abundance of eternal life is a reward.

Are you living today in light of *that* day? By focusing on your eternal payday you will glorify God more now, and you will store up greater wages for eternity.

CHAPTER 3

We Really Do Reap What We Sow
(Galatians 6:6-10)

It was the illustrious, steel-faced coach of the Dallas Cowboys, Tom Landry, who said:

> I've seen the difference character makes in individual football players. Give me a choice between an outstanding athlete with poor character and a lesser athlete of good character, and I'll choose the latter every time. The athlete with good character will often perform to his fullest potential and be a successful football player, while the outstanding athlete with poor character will usually fail to play up to his potential and often won't even achieve average performance.[1]

The key factor in productivity is not ability. It's character that counts. This principle holds true in our Christian lives as well. Only the believer who is humble and continually seeking God's glory will reach his or her potential in life.

All believers have the potential of experiencing the life God has given them in an abundant way. But as we shall see in Galatians 6:6-10, some fail to live up to their potential. They indulge the flesh, grow tired while doing good, and lose heart. And when that occurs, these believers suffer great loss.

---

[1] Edythe Draper, *Draper's Book of Quotations for the Christian World* (Wheaton: Tyndale House Publishers, Inc., 1992). Entries 1017-1019.

The loss they incur answers one of the greatest objections people have to the doctrine of justification by faith alone—that it seems to promote sin. "If I believed that, why wouldn't I go out and live like the devil?" is a question I've heard many times while explaining the good news to people. They have difficulty understanding why a person who knew he was secure eternally would choose to live for God.

Actually, there are a number of compelling reasons for an eternally secure believer to choose to live a godly life. Paul powerfully states one of them in Galatians 6:7:

> Do not be deceived, God is not mocked; for whatever a man sows, that he will also reap.

The problem, as I see it, is that most people simply do not believe this. They rationalize that if those who merely believe in Christ are eternally secure, then they are also free to sin with impunity.

But in reality, the only way anyone can expect to find peace, joy, and contentment is by living life the way God directs. The principle of sowing and reaping applies to all people, including believers.

God Is Not Mocked

The idea that eternally secure people have no reason to live for God inadvertently demonstrates a very low opinion of God, giving the impression that God is powerless to motivate His children to obey Him.

Earthly parents have no ability to threaten their children with hell. Yet good parents are able to motivate their children to obey them. The American government can't send anyone to hell either, but it has many ways of motivating obedience to its laws. Is God less powerful than earthly parents or human government? No one—believer or unbeliever—can live like the devil and "get away with it." That would be mocking God!

On one occasion the prophet Elisha was being mocked by a group of teenage hooligans. His mentor, the prophet Elijah, had just gone up to heaven alive in a whirlwind. Now the youths shouted to Elisha, "Go up, baldhead."

God doesn't often respond to mocking with instant capital punishment, but He did that day. He had Elisha pronounce a curse on the youths. Two bears came out of the woods and mauled forty-two of them to death. God is not mocked with impunity. Sometimes the judgment is immediate. Sometimes it comes later. But it always comes (see 2 Kings 2:23-25).

In Galatians 6:6-10, Paul is not focusing on judgment here and now. The emphasis, as we shall see, is on future judgment at the Judgment Seat of Christ. However, the principle that God is not mocked has application both now and forever. The believer who departs to the proverbial spiritual far country (Luke 15:13) will experience judgment now and then again at the Bema.

Not Free-Gift Language

Galatians 6:6-10 is not a passage about justification by faith alone. Eternal salvation is a free gift (John 4:10; Ephesians 2:8-9; Romans 4:4-5) received by faith alone in Christ alone (John 6:35-40; 11:25-27). And it is a present possession (John 5:24; 6:47).

Therefore, whatever "reaping eternal life" means, it can't contradict other Scripture. What else but eternal rewards could be in view, since those indeed are earned and are future? If Paul were speaking of justification truth, then he, like the Lord Jesus, would refer to having eternal life right now. "He who believes in Me *has* everlasting life" (John 6:47, emphasis mine) is far different from "He who sows to the Spirit *will* of the Spirit *reap* everlasting life" (Galatians 6:8, emphasis mine). The latter passage is neither free-gift language nor present-possession truth.

It is important to keep in mind that whenever eternal life is spoken of as a possible future possession, eternal *rewards* are in view. Whenever eternal life is spoken of as a present possession, then eternal *salvation* is in focus.

Calling *Believers* to Do Good Works

That Paul is not talking about justification by faith in Christ is also supported by his emphasis on works and the absence of any mention of faith. The words "believe" and "faith" occur only once in this passage, and then merely as a reference to the fact that we are to make special effort to help our fellow believers "who are of the household of *faith*" (verse 10). Compare this to Galatians 3:6-14 where the words *believe* (*pisteuō*) and faith (*pistis*) occur ten times to show that the sole condition of justification is faith in Christ.

This paragraph in Galatians 6 begins and ends with calls to do good works. In the first verse of the paragraph (verse 6), there is a call to help those who teach the Bible: "Let him who is taught the word share in all good things with him who teaches." This surely includes financial assistance.

The last two verses in the paragraph (verses 9-10) refer to *doing good*:

> And let us not grow weary while *doing good*, for in due season we shall reap if we do not lose heart. Therefore, as we have opportunity, let us *do good* to all, especially to those who are of the household of faith.

The intervening material (verses 7-8) is also about doing good. We are not to sow to the flesh; rather, we are to sow to the Spirit.

Of course, I realize many well-intentioned people believe that Paul is warning professing believers that if they fail to persevere in good works they will go to hell, since they will have proved to be false professors. Such thinking, however, destroys the freeness of the gospel, eliminates the doctrine of eternal rewards, and, is directly contradicted by the context.

Paul makes it crystal clear that believers should fear losing heart and failing to reap everlasting life. So doesn't this mean that believers can lose eternal salvation? No. As we shall soon see, Paul uses the expression *everlasting life* here to refer to fullness of life forever.

Before we consider the meaning of everlasting life in this passage, it is vital that we observe that Paul's use of the first person plural in verse 9 includes himself. If *we* lose heart, *we* will not reap eternal life. On another occasion (1 Corinthians 9:24-27) he even used the first person singular (compare 2 Timothy 2:12 and 4:7-8). Paul was not sure that he would persevere and gain *the full experience of everlasting life* that goes to those who endure. Yet Paul knew with certainty that he was eternally secure (Galatians 2:15-16; 3:6-14; 2 Timothy 1:12).

A Life Full of Potential

The expression *everlasting life* in the New Testament is used in two different senses. Often it refers to spiritual life that never ends. For example, the Lord Jesus promised that "whoever lives and believes in Me shall never die" (John 11:26).

However, eternal life does not merely refer to unending life. Since eternal life is God's kind of life (Jesus said, "I am the life"), it is a life full of creative potential. As such, it is a life that can be experienced to greater or lesser degrees. Just as there is great range in the way unbelievers utilize their lives, so there is with believers as well.

The Lord Jesus Himself is called "eternal life" by the Apostle John, "And we are in Him who is true, in His Son Jesus Christ. This is the true God and eternal life" (1 John 5:20). The Lord Jesus did not receive life from anyone. To quote John again, "In Him was life" (John 1:4). Because of this, Jesus could say something that no one else could, "I lay down My life that I may take it again...I have power to lay it down, and I have power to take it again" (John 10:17-18). When Jesus rose from the dead, *He raised Himself up.* "Destroy this temple, and in three days I will raise it up" (John 2:19).

Our God-given life is full of potential. A new Christian does not experience the quality of eternal life that a mature believer does. As a person grows in Christ, so does his experience of eternal life. We all know senior saints who are marvelous examples of this. They are experiencing the abundant life of which Jesus spoke, "I have come that they may have life, and that they may have it more abundantly" (John 10:10b). As Jody Dillow noted:

> Eternal life is no static entity but a relationship with God. It is dynamic and growing and has degrees. Some Christians have a more intimate relationship with God than others. They have a richer experience of eternal life.[2]

Galatians 6:8 is the only place in the Bible where we find the expression *reaping eternal life.* However, there are similar expressions in Matthew 19:29 ("inherit everlasting life") and in Luke 18:30 ("receive...in the age to come everlasting life"). In all three of these passages *reaping, inheriting,* and *receiving* eternal life refer to having a *fuller experience of His life* in the future.[3]

---

[2] Joseph C. Dillow, *The Reign of the Servant Kings: A Study of Eternal Security and the Final Significance of Man* (Hayesville, NC: Schoettle Publishing Company, 1992), 140.

[3] See Dillow, 140. He says, "In every place where eternal life is presented as something which can be obtained by works, it is contextually *always* described as a future acquisition. Conversely, whenever eternal life is described as something in the present, it is obtained by faith alone."

Let Us Not Grow Weary

Once we receive the gift of everlasting life, the *fact* of our eternal *existence* as children of God is secure. However, the *quality* of our eternal experience is not secure until we die. All believers will have joy forever, but only some will have *abundant* joy forever. How we live our Christian lives will determine what we reap in the life to come.

God conditions this future harvest upon works. The analogy of sowing and reaping is taken from farming. It takes a lot of effort to plow the ground, sow the seeds, water, weed, and then harvest. Only by persistent hard work will a farmer reap a good crop. So, too, only by persistent hard work will the believer reap an abundant eternal experience (see also 1 Corinthians 9:24-27 and 2 Timothy 2:6).

The quality of life varies greatly among people. Money and possessions are not the decisive factors. We all know of wealthy people whose lives are empty and without direction. And we know others with fewer financial resources whose lives are full and meaningful. What determines quality of life is attitude. In eternity all believers will have significance and direction. Yet some will experience life more fully and serve God to a greater degree.

Galatians 6:9 is a powerful reminder to the believer: "Let us not grow weary while doing good, for in due season we shall reap if we do not lose heart." It's not enough to begin well. Even hanging in there in our service for Christ for decades is not enough. In order to reap, we must endure to the end.

At the 1984 Summer Olympics in Los Angeles, the first women's Olympic marathon was held. One scene from that race stands out above all the rest. The scene to which I refer is not Joan Benoit Samuelson crossing the finish line first. It isn't about someone who won a medal, but about an also-ran.

Gabrielle Andersen-Scheiss, a Swiss-American runner, became ill during the race.[4] By the twenty-four-mile mark she was reduced to an awkward jog. By twenty-five miles she could barely walk. Yet she kept on, determined to finish, even though the race for the medals was long over.

---

[4] For a picture of her from the race and a brief account, see http://www.olympic.org/uk/games/past/facts_uk.asp?OLGT=1&OLGY=1984.

Somehow she made it into the stadium—one lap to go. The TV monitors captured her image. Hundreds of millions of people were aghast. Gabrielle was staggering from one side of the track to the other. Four times in the final lap officials approached her urging her to quit. Four times she awkwardly waved them off. Stumbling across the finish line, she collapsed.[5]

It still brings tears to my eyes when I think of what she did that day. Oh, how I want to finish the Christian life well, in spite of the problems and difficulties ahead!

Conclusion

The reception of eternal life at the point of initial faith in Christ is just the beginning of the Christian life. From that point forward, believers have the opportunity to lay up eternal rewards. We are in the process now of determining the quality of our eternal experience. Make no mistake—effort is involved in order to have a full experience of eternal life now and forever.

While all believers will live in the kingdom, only believers who persist in good works will enjoy a special abundance of life.

All of us are repeatedly tempted to throw in the spiritual towel. The flesh wars against the Spirit and won't quit until we go to be with the Lord (Galatians 5:17). A desire for abundant eternal life should be one motivating factor to keep on keeping on in the Christian life.

Don't give up. Our judgment day, the Judgment Seat of Christ, is coming. A lot is at stake. The quality of our eternal experience hangs in the balance.

---

[5] The story has a happy ending: Gabrielle recovered fully after the race.

Section 2

Who Receives Rewards?

"Well done, good servant;
because you were faithful in a very little,
have authority over ten cities."

Luke 19:17

CHAPTER 4

Faithful Servants
(Luke 19:11-27)

S tacy Dragila, winner of the gold medal in the 2000 Olympics in Sydney, Australia, is one the greatest women's pole-vaulter of all time. She held both the indoor and outdoor world records for years. Eight times in 2001, she set new world records.

In August of 2001 Stacy competed in the International Track and Field Championships in Edmonton, Alberta. She had a good opportunity to win the World Championships, but at no point could she afford to give a half hearted effort. Perseverance is one of the hallmarks of any great athlete. So it is for anyone who wishes to be great in God's service.

Setting the Stage

In the Parable of the Minas found in Luke 19:11-27, the Lord indicates that He is going away (in His death, resurrection, and ascension), leaving His servants with work to do, and then returning to evaluate how each one did. Each of the servants are given one mina, a sum of money equivalent to about $5,000 today.[1] While we know that not all people have the same degree of ability in life, this parable is answering a key question: If three people have equal ability and opportunity, yet they have a wide range of productivity in

---

[1] A mina was equal to three months pay for a day laborer. In the United States, that would be around $5,000 for a minimum wage earner. However, in third-world countries three months wages would be much less.

their service for Christ, how will He evaluate and recompense their varied service?

Let's see how each servant fares in this judgment.

The All-Star

The first person in the parable clearly performed best, multiplying the money the Lord gave him ten times (Luke 19:16). This man maximized his abilities and opportunities.

Surely this is meant to illustrate the believer who serves Christ wholeheartedly throughout his Christian life. Though he wasn't perfect, he gave the Lord his best efforts. His heart was in the right place and he was laying up treasures in heaven, not on earth (Matthew 6:19-21).

The Lord's response to this all-star believer was, "Well done, good servant; because you were faithful in a very little, have authority over ten cities" (Luke 19:17). First, this servant heard, "Well done, good servant." What great words to hear from the King of kings!

Second, he learned about a tangible reward he would receive for his good service: "Have authority over ten cities." Clearly Jesus was speaking of His eternal kingdom here. This type of servant would reign over "ten cities."

Make no mistake. This person was not being told that he would get into the kingdom. Rather, he was being informed about the ministry he would receive when he got there. In the age to come, only the most faithful servants from this life will have major authority in the kingdom.

We should not overlook the fact that this is a grand promotion. The Lord said, "Because you were faithful *in a very little...*" There are many ways we can faithfully serve Christ in this life. The All-Star might be one who serves faithfully for fifty years as an elder in a small rural church. Or it might be a missionary couple who serve in a hostile culture for decades, while seeing very few come to faith in Christ. It might be a widow who had been a wonderful wife and mother and who remains a mainstay in her local church. But whatever ministry he or she has in this life is called "very little" by the Lord in comparison to the ministry that lies ahead.

The Journeyman

In every sport there are professional athletes called journeymen. They play their sport faithfully for many years, yet without distinction. Such people may or may not maximize their talents.

Ryan Leaf was a journeyman quarterback in the pros. In college he had been a star. He was the second player taken in the 1998 draft right after Peyton Manning. Ryan is 6 foot 5, weighs 235, and has a cannon for an arm. Yet in his three years in San Diego, he won very few games. Still, Ryan Leaf accomplished something. He completed 272 passes, 13 for touchdowns. He personally ran the ball 55 times. He played in pain, and also under a lot of criticism.

In the 2001 season he was signed by the Cowboys for the veteran minimum of $500,000, even though it was discovered he had a major problem in his throwing wrist. Why? Because the Cowboys needed additional quarterbacks, and Ryan Leaf might have had something to contribute. Ryan Leaf ended up playing only four years in the NFL. Peyton Manning is entering his seventeenth year. Even a person like Leaf who fails to reach his full potential is rewarded for what he does.

The second servant in the parable is somewhat like a journeyman who fails to maximize his talents. He had the same amount of ability and opportunity as the first servant, as is represented by the one mina with which they each started. But the second servant failed to contribute as much as he could have. "Master, your mina has earned five minas" (Luke 19:18). Not a great return.

While the Lord had no words of praise for him, what He did say was still encouraging: "You also be over five cities" (Luke 19:19). That is a far cry from the praise and authority the first servant received. Yet this second servant would rule with Christ in His kingdom. Five minas resulted in five cities.

Now there are many different ways in which believers might achieve only half of what the Lord has for them to accomplish. Some might serve Him halfheartedly for their entire Christian lives.[2] Others might serve Him wholeheartedly for half of their Christian lives. Still others might run hot and cold again and again.

---

[2] Of course, in order to rule at all the person would have to be walking with Christ *at the time of the Rapture or his death*: "If we endure, we shall also reign with Him" (2 Tim 2:12; se also Gal 6:9; Rev 2:26).

The Scared Shirker

While many suggest that the third servant is an unfaithful unbeliever, the evidence overwhelmingly shows that this servant is
an unfaithful *believer*.[3] First, this person is a servant of Christ.
Unbelievers are not. Second, he is entrusted with something to
invest for his Lord. Unbelievers are not. Third, he is neither rebuked
for lack of faith, nor told that the Lord never knew him. Unbelievers
are (compare Matthew 7:21-23). Fourth, he is clearly contrasted
with unbelievers. Immediately after his judgment we read these
words, "But bring here those enemies of mine, who did not want
me to reign over them [i.e., didn't want to be in a kingdom with
this person as their king], and slay them before me" (verse 27). The
word "but" unequivocally indicates that the third servant was not
part of the group that is slain. Slaying here is figurative for eternal
separation from the kingdom (cf. Revelation 20:14).

I call the third servant a "scared shirker" because of what he did
and how he justified it. He didn't do as the other two servants did,
and invest the money in ventures that generated good returns. He
didn't even put it in the bank where at least it could have earned
some interest. He just hid it.[4]

Here is what he said in his defense:

> "Master, here is your mina, which I have kept put away in a
> handkerchief. For I feared you, because you are an austere
> man. You collect what you did not deposit, and reap what
> you did not sow" (Luke 19:20-21).

---

[3] See Zane C. Hodges, *The Gospel Under Siege*, revised and enlarged edition
(Dallas, TX: Redención Viva, 1981, 1992), 130-32, *A Free Grace Primer* (Denton,
TX, Grace Evangelical Society, 2011), 310-313, and Joseph C. Dillow, *The Reign of
the Servant Kings: A Study of Eternal Security and the Final Significance of Man*
(Hayesville, NC: Schoettle Publishing Company, 1992), 564-65, 589.

[4] Hiding the money would thus represent failure to confess Christ. This person
would be a secret believer like Nicodemus in the Gospel of John. Sadly there are some
believers today who think that they don't need to go to church or be baptized or tell
others about their faith. They figure their faith is a personal matter. Unfortunately,
they are burying that which God expects them to invest in His service.

The Lord said that at the very least this servant should have invested the money He
gave him in the bank. What does that represent? Well, this servant failed to confess
Christ. Thus the very least he could have done would have been to give the money so
that others could do what he would not—evangelize and disciple.

What he is saying is that he feared doing something wrong and losing the mina altogether. He knew that the Lord was holding him accountable and wanted a return on the money He had given him.

Bishop W. C. Magee once said, "The man who makes no mistakes usually does not make anything." It is true that if you don't take any risks in life, you probably won't have any big losses. But you also won't accomplish much.

If the third servant was so concerned about pleasing his master, why didn't he put the money in the bank to earn at least a small return?

We mustn't conclude that this type of person never did even one good work.[5] Surely only believers who die at the moment of regeneration will do absolutely no good works. It merely means the person failed to come up with even a minimal return on investment.

What is the return in view? In many other places in Scripture, ruling with Christ is conditioned upon ongoing confession of Christ (e.g., 2 Timothy 2:12; Hebrews 10:23). A person may do good works, yet without confessing his faith in Christ. Thus the minimal return required is persevering in open confession of our faith in Christ.

There are many ways in which we may confess our faith in Christ. Evangelism is one way. Telling others we are Christians, which is really pre-evangelism, is another. Going to church and serving there are other ways in which we identify ourselves as believers (Hebrews 10:23-25). Baptism is certainly a public testimony of our faith (Matthew 28:18-20). And when we disciple other believers, we are professing our faith in Christ to them, and to anyone who knows we are teaching others about Christ.

In a sense, any ministry we do in and through the local church is professing Christ. To be at least a Journeyman, we must make our faith in Christ public. However, to be an All-Star, we need to do more than simply show others that we are Christians. We must *maximize* our time, talent, and treasure for Christ. Half-hearted service will not result in the commendation, "Well done, good servant."

The minas represent the time, talent, and treasure God has given us to serve Him by ministering to others in His name. It is thus

---

[5] Ibid. Hodges says, "Whether or not he did other commendable things is not the point of the parable."

fitting that for each mina earned, the servant gains authority over another city in the life to come. Our level of authority in the coming life will be directly related to our ministry to people in this life.

Pursuing the Prize

Stacy Dragila won the gold medal in the 2001 World Championships. Interestingly, the second place competitor actually cleared the same height. Stacy won because she had fewer misses at lower heights. Her persistence in training paid off.

When athletes look back on their careers, all they can hope for is to have done the best with their God-given abilities. The same is true of the Christian. Our aim should be to have His full approval when we reach the end of our lives. We should want to maximize our lives for Christ so that we will hear those blessed words, "Well done, good servant." Oh, to hear those words from the One who means so much to us.

CHAPTER 5

Loving Disciples
(1 John 2:28; 4:17-19)

Many Christians don't realize that they may feel shame when they stand before Christ at His Judgment Seat. Yet, we will have confidence before Him at His coming only if we abide in Him. The believer who makes himself at home with the world and not with Christ, will be ashamed of himself on that day:

And now, little children, abide in Him, that when He appears, we may have confidence and not be ashamed before Him at His coming (1 John 2:28).[1]

In his commentary on the Johannine epistles, Zane Hodges discusses confidence and shame at the Bema:

Even though eternal salvation is an entirely free gift which can never be lost, the New Testament makes plain that the believer must give an account of his or her Christian life in the presence of Christ (cf. 2 Corinthians 5:10; Romans 14:10-12)…Therefore, shame is decidedly possible at the Judgment Seat. This is all the more true since Christians at that time will have their eternal bodies. Thus sin will no longer inhibit appropriate regret and embarrassment about

---

[1] Technically, John includes himself (note the shift from *you* in the command to *we* in the result clause), as experiencing same along with the readers if they did not abide. However, clearly it is the readers who would be ashamed of themselves if they were not abiding when Christ returned.

those things in one's earthly life that did not please the
Lord.[2]

Instead of shame, the Apostle John suggests that his readers can
have *confidence...before Him at His coming.* "Confidence" translates a Greek word (*parrēsia*) that may also mean "boldness" or
"fearlessness." Such an experience in the presence of our Lord at
His review of our lives is earnestly to be desired.

Some believers live as though they couldn't possibly experience
shame before Christ. After all, sins are supposed to be forgiven,
right?

It is true, of course, that the Lord Jesus by His death on the cross
took away all of our sins, past, present, and future (John 1:29; 1
John 2:2). Sin is no longer a barrier to anyone having eternal salvation. The moment we believe in Jesus for eternal life, He gives it to
us. Eternal life, however, does not exclude accountability. Believers
still need fellowship forgiveness (1 John 1:9). And if a believer is
out of fellowship with God when his life is over, he will experience
shame at the Bema.

Fear Is Sometimes Appropriate

My mother-in-law, Camille, panicked every time she saw a police
car on the highway. I don't normally share her fear, unless I am
doing something wrong!

The same principle applies in relationships. A child raised in a
good home need not fear rebuke if he is doing what his parents ask.
A student in school who is obeying the teacher's rules need not fear
detention. A hardworking employee who is abiding by the office
regulations has no reason to fear being put on probation.

The knowledge that actions have consequences motivates us to
do right. Many Christians don't stop to think that the same is true
in our relationship with God. If we are busy doing what He wants
us to do, manifesting His love to others, we need not fear discipline
now or rebuke at the Judgment Seat of Christ.

One of the most powerful statements by the Apostle John is
that "perfect love casts out fear" (1 John 4:18). In fact, it is even
more powerful when it is properly understood in the context of the

---

[2] Zane C. Hodges, *The Epistles of John: Walking in the Light of God's Love* (Denton,
TX: Grace Evangelical Society, 1999), 125.

Judgment Seat of Christ and the need for love to be perfected in our hearts.

In 1 John 4:17 the Apostle writes,

> Love has been perfected among us in this: *that we may have boldness in the day of judgment*; because as He is, so are we in this world (emphasis mine).

There is only one *day of judgment* for the Christian. That is the Bema, or the Judgment Seat of Christ.

Christians will never be judged to determine our eternal destiny (John 5:24). That was settled the moment we believed in Christ (John 3:18). Yet we *will* be judged. The purpose of the Bema is to recompense believers for work done, whether good or bad (2 Corinthians 5:10).

If we miss this simple fact, we get the wrong impression about where this verse is heading.

Mature Love Leads to Boldness

What might John mean by "love has been perfected among [or in] us"? Zane Hodges's comments on this verse are helpful:

> God's love is not *perfected* in a Christian whose heart is simply a reservoir in which to receive it, but only in a Christian whose heart furnishes an aqueduct to convey it to others.[3]

The word "boldness" in 1 John 4:17 is the same Greek word (*parrēsia*) that is translated "confidence" in 2:28, the theme verse for the letter. Believers who abide in Christ will have confidence and boldness when He appears; they will not shrink back in shame at Christ's coming.[4]

Here John concludes this theme. Believers in whom God's love has been perfected will have boldness at the Bema. Like obedient children of good parents, we have nothing to fear. We can and should be confident, for our Lord is a Judge who is loving, gracious, and fair. He will commend believers in whom His love has matured.

---

[3] Ibid., 198-99, emphasis his.

[4] There is a play on words here in Greek that is missed in English. The word for Christ's coming is *parousia*. It rhymes with the word for boldness, *parrēsia*. John wants us to have *parrēsia* at the *parousia*.

Perfect Love Casts Out Fear

John goes on to say,

> There is no fear in love; but perfect love casts out fear, because fear involves torment. But he who fears has not been made perfect in love (1 John 4:18).

This is commonly misunderstood as referring to assurance of salvation. It is thought that if I am sure of God's perfect love for me, then I have no fear of eternal condemnation. Yet this verse is about "the day of judgment" at the Bema, which all believers indeed will face. And it concerns our manifesting God's love to others, not about Him manifesting His love toward us.

John's point is that loving Christians need not fear the Bema. However, a believer who is not mature in love should reasonably fear his coming day of judgment before the Lord.

John is calling us to make loving others our aim in life. He made this point forcefully in 1 John 3:16-23. There he says, "Let us not love in word or in tongue [i.e., Let's not just *talk* about love], but in deed and in truth" (3:18). God's love is active in us only if we are giving of our energy and possessions to help others (3:16-17). And the more we love, by abiding in Christ, the better our judgment will be at His Judgment Seat.

When John says, "Perfect love casts out fear, *because fear involves torment*," he is not talking about eternal torment in hell. John is speaking to believers here ("Beloved," 4:1, 7, 11; compare 2:2, 12-14, 26). The words translated "involves torment" (*kolasin echei*) would be better translated as "has punishment" or "is punishment." The idea is that fear is itself a form of divine punishment or discipline.[5] God disciplines us so that we will learn and get back on track. If we respond properly to God's discipline, then we will grow and become more loving. That in turn eliminates the fear.

Some Christians experience false guilt. John has a remedy for such people and it's basically this: chill out.

> If our heart condemns us [that we are not loving and hence not abiding in the truth of God], God is greater than our heart, and knows all things. Beloved if our heart

---

[5] Hodges, *The Epistles of John*, 202.

does not condemn us, we have confidence toward God (1 John 3:20-21).

The believer who doesn't *feel* confident about the coming judgment at the Bema, but yet who is walking in fellowship with Christ, should realize that God will take into account all of the loving deeds we have done. It is comforting to realize that we may be harder on ourselves than the Lord Jesus will be.

Gratitude Can Produce Mature Love

John ends the body of his epistle with these marvelous words, "We love Him because He first loved us" (1 John 4:19). Believe it or not, this is the first time in the epistle that John speaks directly of our love for God.

What moves us to love God? It is His love for us! Gratitude is a powerful motivator.

Mature love develops as we grow to appreciate what God has done for us in Christ. It all starts with Him. Jesus told His disciples, "Without Me you can do nothing" (John 15:5).[6]

I used to think that we could live the Christian life by commitment of the will; that we could please God by trying hard. Then I came to see that what God wants from us is faith in Him. Our lives are transformed only by the renewing of our minds (Romans 12:1-2). And mind renewal starts with loving God. If we don't love God, no amount of commitment can produce godliness. Commitment without love produces legalism.

Conclusion

As the Apostle John shows, our coming day of judgment should powerfully motivate us to grow and mature in our love for one another.

Mature love casts out fear of the Bema. If you live each day in light of *that* day, God's love will become more mature in you. The

---

[6] The idea of abiding in Christ and having mature love is found throughout the Upper Room Discourse (John 13–16). See especially John 14:15 ("If you love Me, keep My commandments") and 15:12-14, 17 ("This is My commandment, that you love one another as I have loved you. Greater love has no one than this, than to lay down one's life for his friends. You are my friends if you do whatever I command you…These things I command you, that you love one another").

people around you will be blessed. God will be glorified. And you will have reason to look toward the Bema with confidence.

CHAPTER 6

Nike Christians
(2 Timothy 1:11-13)

The one word that best describes Thomas Alva Edison is *persistent.* Certainly he would never have invented the modern lightbulb and numerous other inventions if he had been one to give up.

The first electric light was actually invented in 1800 by an English scientist, Sir Humphry Davy. By connecting wires to a battery and hooking the wires up to carbon, Davy produced an electric arc.

By 1879 various efforts at making electric lights had been tried in England and America, but no one had come up with a type of filament that would conduct electricity, glow, and yet not burn up quickly. Edison tried hundreds of possible filaments, with failure being the one constant. Before he finally found something that would work, he experienced over 900 failures in a row! But Edison knew that the prize was well worth the effort and the frustration.

Finally he discovered that a carbon filament in an oxygen-free bulb glowed for forty hours before going out. He eventually produced a bulb that could glow for over 1,500 hours.

I grew up in Southern California where the electric company is called Southern California Edison. His name is one of the most recognizable in our world today. He gained prestige, honor, fame, and wealth for himself and his heirs.

His fame was not the result of his birth (his father was a carpenter), his education (his teachers thought he was a poor student), or good luck. Believing that persistent hard work paid off, Edison worked many twenty-hour days. He often said, "Genius is one percent inspiration and ninety-nine percent perspiration."

Because of Edison's unwavering commitment and perseverance, he became one of the most prolific inventors of all time, patenting an amazing 1,093 inventions.

Wouldn't it be great if that same commitment to hard work and perseverance characterized our Christian lives? It can. The recognition that our perseverance pleases God, and will ultimately result in the privilege of ruling with Christ, can motivate such persistence.

Eternal Life Is Absolutely Secure

Second Timothy 2:11-13 is a passage that stresses both the freeness of eternal salvation and the costliness of eternal rewards.

> *For if we died with Him,*
> *We shall also live with Him.*
> *If we endure,*
> *We shall also reign with Him.*
> *If we deny Him,*
> *He also will deny us.*
> *If we are faithless,*
> *He remains faithful;*
> *He cannot deny Himself.*

Similar to the four-inch newspaper headlines that proclaimed the end of WW II on VE (Victory in Europe) Day, verses 11 and 13 clearly and forcefully proclaim news of great victory. By virtue of their union with Christ, every Christian is secure forever. It's a done deal that can't be reversed, even by faithlessness on the part of the believer.

Verse 11 says, "If we died with Him, we shall also live with Him." This is another way of saying that every believer has eternal life and can never lose it. If we have believed in Christ for eternal life, then we have died with Him in a positional sense (Romans 6:5, 8; Galatians 2:20; 5:24). By *positional* I mean that God views us as though we died with Jesus on the cross. While in our *experience* we did not die with Christ, God in His grace credits us with having been crucified with Christ.[1]

---

[1] Since God credits us with dying with Christ, He also changes our nature. Believers are no longer slaves of sin (Romans 6:7). Rather, born again people are

Three days after He died, the Lord Jesus rose again. Implicit in Paul's statement in verse 11 is the understanding that we who died with Him also rose with Him (see Ephesians 2:6). However, Paul's focus is beyond even our co-resurrection with Christ. His focus is on living with Him forever—"we shall also live with Him."

Just as there is no question that Jesus is eternally secure, so all who died with Him are secure as well. There is no escape clause. There is no such thing as one who has died with Christ but who will fail to live with Him forever.

As verse 13 says, "If we are faithless, He remains faithful; He cannot deny Himself." Jesus promises everlasting life to all who believe in Him. *Our* faithfulness is not part of the equation. It is *His* faithfulness that guarantees that we stay saved. Since He will always be faithful to that which He promised, all believers, including faithless ones, will live with Christ forever.

Paul knew, however, that faithfulness matters to God. Eternal security is not a license to lethargy. Verse 12 reveals the consequences for both *faithfulness* and *faithlessness*. First, Paul considers the consequences for faithfulness.

Christians Who Endure

Even a casual reading of the passage shows that verse 12 is discussing something different than verses 11 and 13. While those verses are extremely comforting and encouraging to all believers, verse 12 is comforting and encouraging only to those believers who are currently walking in fellowship with God.

Verse 12a reads, "If we endure, we shall also reign with Him." Paul had spoken of his own endurance, using the same Greek verb, in verse 10. There it clearly refers to persevering in the faith in spite of persecution and suffering (verse 9). If other Christians would follow his example and endure in the faith in spite of persecution and suffering, then they too would rule with Christ.

---

slaves of righteousness (Romans 6:18). This means that we no longer need to live the way we once did. Of course, success is not guaranteed simply because we have the ability to obey. The believers in Corinth were still living like the unsaved five years after their new birth (1 Corinthians 3:3). It should be noted that Paul is not bringing out this aspect of our co-crucifixion with Christ. For in this context he is stressing the security associated with our death with Christ.

Some mistakenly think that reigning with Christ is synonymous with being a Christian. However, Paul makes it clear in this passage that while all Christians—including faithless ones—have life, only persevering Christians will rule with Christ.

The Lord Jesus also made it clear that only overcoming Christians will rule with Him (compare Luke 19:16-26; Revelation 2:26; 3:21). While all Christians will be in His kingdom, only those who endure in this life will be a part of His kingdom administration. Since serving Christ is what we will do in eternity (Revelation 22:3), increased opportunity to serve Him should be extremely desirable. What a privilege to serve the King of kings by being a ruler over a city, county, state, or even country.[2]

While eternal life is free, eternal rulership will cost us persistent hard work: "if we endure, we shall also reign with Him."

Christians Who Deny Christ

"If we deny Him, He also will deny us." Some think that Paul is threatening believers who deny Christ with eternal damnation. That, however, is completely contrary to the first half of verse 12 and to the context of verses 11 and 13.

The second half of verse 12 is antithetically parallel to the first half. After the words, "If we endure, we shall also reign with Him," we expect, "If we don't endure, we shall not reign with Him." Yet that is precisely what verse 12b *is* saying. To deny Christ is to fail to endure in the faith. To be denied by Him is to be refused the privilege of ruling with Him.

Why didn't Paul just keep it simple by saying, "If we fail to endure, we won't reign"? It would seem that he is using the second half of verse 12 to paraphrase the Lord Jesus' words recorded in Matthew 10:33, "But whoever denies Me before men, him I will also deny before My Father who is in heaven."

At the Judgment Seat, the Lord Jesus will confess those believers who have openly confessed Him before others. "Therefore whoever confesses Me before men, him I will also confess before My Father who is in heaven" (Matthew 10:32). Thus Paul's implicit exhortation to endure in the first half of verse 12 includes the idea of confessing

---

[2] Rulership probably will also include management that we don't normally think of as political. See Chapter 10, especially the section "Rulers in the Life to Come," for a discussion of other types of ruling with Christ.

Christ before others. Probably the reason Paul spoke of enduring rather than confessing is because endurance suggests obedience on many fronts, including acknowledging Christ.

All who endure in their Christian lives will rule with Christ. However, as the second half of the verse brings out, endurance in confessing Christ is the *minimum* requirement. If one merely endures in his profession of Christ, he will rule.[3] However, Paul is calling for more than minimal endurance and reward. He wants Timothy, and all of us, to excel in the Christian life now and in rulership in the life to come.

Sadly, not all Christians openly confess Christ. Surely all of us have failed at this from time to time, but what Paul has in mind is a believer who has ceased to name the name of Christ publicly. If before we die or are raptured, we have become silent about our faith, we will not be confessed by Christ and we will not rule with Him.

How can a believer deny Christ before others? One obvious way is to cease going to church. Church is a very public way in which believers confess the name of Christ (Hebrews 10:23-25).

We err if we think this passage primarily relates to passing out gospel tracts or doing door-to-door evangelism. While those are forms of confessing Christ, neither was done at the time of Christ and Paul. Rather, what is obvious is that when the name of Jesus is mentioned, we must not shrink back as Peter did when he claimed he didn't know Jesus on the night of His betrayal. We must not live like Nicodemus, a member of the Sanhedrin who was a secret disciple of Christ (John 19:38-39). We should be open followers of Christ.

Who will be fit to reign with Christ? Only believers who endure in their confession of Him.

Be a Nike Christian

Coach Bill Bowerman was a legend at the University of Oregon. Steve Prefontaine, one of America's greatest distance runners, rose to prominence under Bowerman's direction.

---

[3] He will rule provided he doesn't disqualify himself by willful indulgence in sin as Galatians 5:19-21 shows.

In 1964 Bowerman teamed with one of his former students, Phil Knight, to form a company called Blue Ribbon Sports.

Eight years later, with Knight at the helm as President and CEO, Blue Ribbon Sports became Nike, Inc. named after the Greek goddess of victory.[4]

The expression "He who overcomes" (Revelation 2:26; 3:21), actually translates the Greek verb, *nikaō,*[5] the noun form of the word *nikē*. The verb and noun refer to winning, being victorious, and overcoming an opponent.

Before he died in a tragic automobile accident at the age of twenty-four, Steve Prefontaine used to speak to crowds of young athletes. "To give anything less than your best is to sacrifice the gift" became one of his famous appeals. On Nike's website you used to find these words, "It was his spirit that helped set our course."[6]

The Nike swoosh has come to symbolize victory. For Nike, doing one's best *is* victory. The same should be true of every Christian; we are winners if we do our best for Jesus Christ.[7]

A Nike Christian is an overcomer, one who perseveres in faith and good works. That is what we are called to be. The Holy Spirit enables all believers to be victorious (2 Peter 1:3), but victory is not automatic. We must be doers of the Word, and not hearers only, if we are to be Nike Christians (James 1:22).

The Apostle Paul often related the Christian life to athletic competition. As he faced execution for his faith he wrote, "I have fought the good fight, I have finished the race, I have kept the faith" (2 Timothy 4:7). That was Paul's aim (see 1 Corinthians 9:24-27), and it should be the aim of every Christian.

Whenever you see the Nike name, I hope you will call to mind its meaning—*overcomer*. And let that remind you that Jesus is coming soon and His reward is with Him (Revelation 22:12). Never

---

[4] The history of Nike, Inc. can be found at their website (nikebiz.com).

[5] The actual expression in Greek is *ho nikōn*. It is a substantive participle that functions as a noun. This can be translated "the one who overcomes," or even, "the victor" or "the winner." Jesus wants every Christian to be a winner in life.

[6] http://www.runningwarehouse.com/nike/nikeinrun.html

[7] There are degrees of overcomers. All who endure are overcomers. But since it is possible to do less than our best, some overcomers will be more highly rewarded than others. Compare verses 17 and 19 in Luke 19 to see the different commendation and reward given to two overcomers, one who maximized his life, and one who was halfhearted in his service.

forget that victorious Christians will rule with Christ. So be a Nike Christian!

CHAPTER 7

Cross Bearers
(Matthew 16:24-28)

The 1993 movie *Indecent Proposal* didn't do too well at the box office. Many moviegoers missed it. So did I. However, it had an interesting premise. According to the movie plot summary:

> A young couple very much in love are married and have started their respective careers...When the recession hits, they stand to lose everything they own, so they go to Vegas to have one shot at winning the money they need. After losing at the tables, they are approached by a millionaire who offers them a million dollars for a night with the wife.

I understand that the couple agreed to this indecent proposal. Under the right circumstances and with the right amount of money, they caved in to immorality. In other words, they could be bought.

Justification by Self-Denial?

A few years ago I received an e-mail message inviting me to check out a dissertation on Jesus' method of evangelism. That dissertation included a section on the Lord's gospel message where the author discussed the passage we are considering. He wrote:

> The teachings of Christ in Matthew 16:24-28 (cf. Luke 9:23-34) make it clear that self-denial, an essential of obedience, is necessary for finding salvation...

So, then, faith and obedience are taught by the Lord not only as ways to eternal life, but as requirements. In order for a man to inherit eternal life he must: believe in Jesus and practice obedience to God.[1]

That is a remarkable claim. Is faith in Christ the only condition of eternal salvation? Or, are self-denial and obedience to God's commands also required, as this writer suggests? Let's look at the entire passage:

Then Jesus said to His disciples, "If anyone desires to come after Me, let him deny himself, and take up his cross, and follow Me. For whoever desires to save his life will lose it, and whoever loses his life for My sake will find it. For what is a man profited if he gains the whole world, and loses his own soul? Or what will a man give in exchange for his soul? For the Son of Man will come in the glory of His Father with His angels, and then He will reward each according to his works. Assuredly, I say to you, there are some standing here who shall not taste death till they see the Son of Man coming in His kingdom" (Matthew 16:24-28).

While I don't agree with the interpretations of Matthew 16:24-28 in that dissertation, I can understand why someone might draw those conclusions. Admittedly, this passage does seem to present a different gospel than John 3:16, which conditions eternal life solely on believing in Christ. Here we find the need to deny oneself, take up one's cross, and follow Christ. This passage also seems to contradict verses like Ephesians 2:8-9, which says that salvation is "not of works, lest anyone should boast." Yet Matthew 16:27 says, "He will reward each *according to his works*" (emphasis mine).

What gives here? We know that Scripture cannot contradict itself. The Bible is God's Word and is completely consistent.

The Meaning of *Psychē*

A proper understanding of the usage of the Greek word *psychē*, is crucial in order to correctly interpret this passage.

---

[1] Paul S. Dixon, *The Evangelism of Christ: A Model for Evangelism Today*, Section 3 ("The Beliefs of Christ Regarding Evangelism"), under "The Requirements of Both Faith and Obedience." See http://solochristo.com/theology/em/PaulDixon_ TheEvangelismofChrist.html.

Psychē appears four times in these verses. Twice it is translated as "life" and twice as "soul." This unfortunate translation decision causes the English reader to think that a different Greek word is being used and a different meaning intended.

Here are those four uses with the Greek word *psychē* inserted instead of its translation:

(1) Whoever desires to save his *psychē* will lose it.

(2) Whoever loses his *psychē* for Christ's sake will find it.

(3) What is a man profited if he gains the whole world and loses his own *psychē*?

(4) What will a man give in exchange for his *psychē*?

What did the Lord mean here by the expression *saving* (or *losing*) *one's psychē*?

Some, like the writer of the dissertation, understand the expression *saving one's psychē* here and in the parallel texts in Matthew 10:38, Mark 8:34, and Luke 9:23 and 14:27, to refer to obtaining eternal salvation from hell. One author writes, "There is no salvation apart from cross-bearing."[2] Another writes, "Thus in a sense we pay the ultimate price for salvation when our sinful self is nailed to a cross. It is total abandonment of self-will....It denotes implicit obedience, full surrender to the lordship of Christ."[3]

Salvation Is Not for Sale

Others, including myself, understand this expression quite differently here and in the parallel texts. There are three major reasons why the eternal salvation view is untenable.

---

[2] James Montgomery Boice, *Christ's Call to Discipleship* (Chicago, IL: Moody Press, 1986), 36.

[3] John F. MacArthur, Jr., *The Gospel According to Jesus: What Does Jesus Mean When He Says, "Follow Me"?* (Grand Rapids, MI: Zondervan Publishing House, 1988), 140. N.B. In the second and third editions (Grand Rapids, MI: Zondervan Publishing House, 1994, 2008), 147, the wording is slightly different, but the message is the same.

Self-denial and Cross-bearing Are Not Gospel Terms

Nowhere in Scripture is eternal salvation conditioned upon self-denial and cross-bearing. Justification is unmerited. It is by grace through faith, not of works (Ephesians 2:9; Romans 4:1-5; Titus 3:5).

Believers Already Have Eternal Life

The disciples (and especially Peter), are being addressed here. They were already believers (Matthew 16:16-17; see also John 2:11).[4] Since eternal salvation can't be lost (John 6:35-40; 10:27-30), the Lord must be warning the disciples about the possibility of losing something else.

Some might wonder how the disciples could have eternal life prior to the cross. After all, eternal redemption had not yet been purchased. However, 2,000 years before the cross, "Abraham believed God, and it was accounted to him for righteousness" (Genesis 15:6; Romans 4:3). God applied the work of the cross to anyone who believed in the Messiah for everlasting life—even before Jesus died. No strings attached.

Eternal Life Is Not a Recompense for Deeds Done

Recompense according to one's deeds (Matthew 16:27) is *not* a justification concept. Rather, it is a rewards concept. Jesus said, "For the Son of Man will come in the glory of His Father with His angels, *and then He will reward each according to his works*" (emphasis mine). Compare especially 2 Corinthians 5:10, a passage that clearly deals with a future works judgment of people who are already eternally secure. It reads:

> *For we must all appear before the judgment seat of Christ,* that each one may receive the things done in the body, *according to what he has done, whether good or bad* (emphasis added).

Eternal life is absolutely free. Eternal rewards are not.

This leads us to the crucial question: What, then, is the Lord Jesus talking about when He speaks of saving one's *psychē*?

---

[4] Judas, of course, never came to faith in Christ and was an example of an unbelieving disciple. Among the twelve, he was the only one who wasn't a believer (see John 13:10).

Developing Our Eternal Capacity

The expression *saving the psychē* in both the Septuagint and the Greek New Testament often refers to preserving one's physical life[5] or to gaining eternal rewards.[6]

All believers have eternal life. However, only self-denying believers will realize *the full potential of eternal life* both in this life and in the life to come (John 10:10; 1 Timothy 4:8).

Suffering precedes glory in God's plan. It did for our Lord and it will for His followers as well. If any believer wants to share fully in Christ's glory when He returns with His angels (verse 27), then suffering for Him now is imperative. We must give to receive. We must lose to gain.

Jesus told the disciples that some of them would not taste death until they saw Him coming in His kingdom (verse 28). We learn in the verses that follow (Matthew 17:1-8) that the three disciples who were closest to Jesus—Peter, James, and John—*did* see Him coming in His kingdom a week later when He was transformed in their presence on the Mount of Transfiguration.

They saw Him in a way they never had before because His glory had been hidden from them. Now they caught a glimpse of what He looked like: "His face shone like the sun, and His clothes became as white as the light" (Matthew 17:2).

The degree to which Jesus will share His glory with believers is related to how much we give of ourselves now. Peter later wrote,

> But rejoice to the extent that you partake of Christ's sufferings, that when His glory is revealed, you may also be glad with exceeding joy (1 Peter 4:13, emphasis added).

Peter had seen a foretaste of that glory and he knew what was at stake. Any time a believer suffers in order to obey and serve God, he is losing his life that he may gain it.

---

[5] Compare Psalm 22:20-21; Proverbs 16:17; Ezekiel 18:27; Matthew 2:20; 20:28; Acts 27:37; 1 Peter 3:20; James 5:19-20.

[6] Compare Colossians 3:23-24; 1 Peter 1:9; Revelation 12:11; 20:4. All of the verses cited here and in n. 5 contain the Greek word *psychē*. However, in the English translations the word *soul* is often not present. Many times the word *life* is given instead. This, of course, supports the point being made here that saving the *psychē* doesn't refer to eternal salvation from hell. In addition, it should be noted that in some of these passages the words *save* or *lose* are not present. However, in each case the *concept* of saving or losing the life is present.

Dr. Earl Radmacher illustrates this concept with cups. Some hold a lot. Others, like demitasse cups, hold very little. In this life we are developing our capacity to serve God. Believers who give up their lives for Christ develop a large capacity to serve and to live.

Application

How can a believer lose his life (i.e., deny himself and take up his cross) for the sake of Christ? By sharing in our Lord's sufferings.

One of the most common ways that committed believers suffer is through the pain we feel from living in this sinful world. Lot was called *righteous* by Peter because the wickedness around him "tormented his righteous soul day to day by seeing and hearing their lawless deeds" (2 Peter 2:8). Similarly Paul said, "For I consider that the sufferings of this present time are not worthy to be compared with the glory which shall be revealed in us" (Romans 8:18). Also, "...we ourselves groan within ourselves, eagerly waiting for the adoption, the redemption of our body" (Romans 8:23).

The *world* says that you can never have enough. The *Word* says that in order to gain a full experience of life you must give up living primarily for the present. In doing so, you may experience suffering. People at work may ridicule you because you share your faith, because your language is different, and you don't laugh at some of their jokes.

Your house and possessions may not be as grand as they could be because you give sacrificially to the Lord's work. You may pay more in taxes than others who make the same salary and deductions, because you don't cheat. You may give up much if you leave parents and hometown to serve the Lord in other parts of the country or abroad. You may even be martyred for your testimony.

If you could possess the wealth of the entire world for the rest of your life on the condition that you sacrifice the quality of your experience in God's kingdom forever, would you do it? Can you be bought?

In order to have a full experience of life now and forever, we must willingly give up our lives in service to God. The world may call us fools. But as martyred missionary Jim Elliot wrote in a now famous journal entry, "He is no fool who gives what he cannot keep to gain that which he cannot lose."[7]

---

[7] The journal entry was from October 28, 1949, six years and a little more than a month before he was martyred by the Auca Indians in Ecuador on January 8, 1956 at the age of 28. A photocopy of the actual journal entry can be found at http://www. wheaton.edu/bgc/archives/faq/20.htm.

CHAPTER 8

Humble Followers
(Luke 17:7-10)

On August 14, 2001 the Dallas Cowboys released starting quarterback Tony Banks. Among other things, he was asked by reporters if he hadn't turned down more money elsewhere to play with the Cowboys in the first place. He indicated that he chose Dallas not for the money, but for the chance to start and prove himself. He said, "That's the only reason I was playing for pennies, because I thought I was going to get a fair shake."

At the time, Banks's salary was $500,000 per year. While that isn't much for an NFL starting quarterback, most people would love to earn that many "pennies" every year. A few years at that level should set someone for life.

In the old days of professional sports, players had jobs in the off-season to supplement their salaries. They were truly playing for the love of the game.

Today, many professional athletes seem to view their exorbitant salaries as their due and not as a wonderful blessing. This is unfortunate. It has resulted in many becoming arrogant, aloof and, in many cases, less than fully committed to doing their best.

Christians must beware of this same trap. We may wonder why we are suffering so much as believers. Why don't we have more money, better houses, finer clothes, newer cars, etc.?

Servants of Christ should avoid developing an entitlement mentality. We are to be humble and self-effacing. Jesus spoke of the need of His servants to have such an attitude in Luke 17:7-10.

Some understand this passage to mean that there will be no eternal rewards. However, the Lord is not denying here that He will reward faithfulness on the part of His servants. Instead, He is talking about what sort of attitude we, as His servants, should have.

We Are His Servants

After teaching the disciples about the need to forgive others (Luke 17:1-4) and to believe Him more (Luke 17:5-6), that is, to believe more of what He says in His Word, the Lord taught them about the proper attitude His servants should have (verses 7-10).

When a servant came in from the field late in the afternoon, his master said, "Prepare something for my supper, and gird yourself and serve me till I have eaten and drunk, and afterward you will eat and drink" (Luke 17:8).

The Lord then asked, "Does he thank that servant because he did the things that were commanded him? I think not" (verse 9). The word translated "thank" could also be translated as "favor" or even "reward." It is the famous word *charis* that is often translated as "grace." The question means something like this, "Did he *show favor toward* [reward] that servant because he did the things that were commanded?"

What's going on here? Does the Lord mean that masters should not thank or reward their servants? Or, to put it in a modern context, that employers shouldn't thank and reward their employees when they do a good job? Of course not.

We have the Lord's teaching backwards if we see the lesson directed to what the masters/employers should do or what their attitude should be. Rather, He was focusing on what the attitude of His servants should be. All believers are servants of Christ. What attitude then should a servant of Christ have concerning rewards?

A Servant Should Serve Humbly

The proper attitude we should have is given in the last verse.

> "So likewise you, when you have done all things which you are commanded, say, 'We are unprofitable servants. We have done what was our duty to do'" (Luke 17:10).

God *does not need to obligate Himself to reward us.* We are His servants and He could simply require us to serve, and discipline us when we don't.

Yet God *does obligate Himself.* He chooses to give rewards. This is demonstrated in many other passages. In Luke 19:17, the Lord says, "Well done, good servant; because you were faithful in a very little, have authority over ten cities." That is both praise and reward. Or, in Revelation 22:12, "And behold, I am coming quickly, and My reward is with Me, to give to every one according to his work." There is no doubt that the Lord Jesus will reward His servants.

May we never forget that the best thing anyone can say about us is that we are servants of the Lord Jesus Christ. That will be our eternal vocation (Revelation 22:3). Whether or not we receive rewards, our status does not change. Now and forever we will serve the King of kings and Lord of lords. That is an exciting future, because being His servant is better than anything else we could possibly do.

Conclusion

Mrs. Lamb was probably the best first grade teacher anyone has ever had. As her student, I was responsible to complete the assignments that she gave me. She didn't have to reward good work with anything other than grades, but she did. She heaped praise on all of us in her class when we did well. There was always a candy bar waiting each time we finished reading another book. And the neatest thing is that she would put us on her lap in front of the whole class and just make a big fuss over the fact that we'd read another book.

That wonderful teacher made me want to come to school. I longed to receive her praise. How much more wonderful it will be to hear the praise of the Lamb of God who took away my sins by shedding His blood on Calvary.

While the Lord will reward believers, He is obligated to do so only because He *chooses* to obligate Himself. That He does so should motivate us to honor Him that much more.

Haughtiness is one of the things God hates most (Proverbs 6:16-17). Humility before God is crucial for the one who wishes to be rewarded. What a blessing it is that God chooses to reward His humble servants.

We should all serve Him regardless of any reward we might obtain. He has done so much for us that we should be overflowing with gratitude and delight in serving such a wonderful Master.

Isn't it great to know that the Lord is not only our Master, but our Friend as well, if we obey Him (John 15:14)? And isn't it encouraging to know there will be praise and reward for those who have served Him well?

I'd serve Him without any eternal rewards. I trust you would as well. But knowing that there will be rewards should heighten our love for Him and our motivation to do our duty.

Section 3
What Are the Rewards?

"If we endure,
we shall also reign with Him."

2 Timothy 2:12a

CHAPTER 9

Heavenly Treasure

Star athlete, heir to a large fortune, and top graduate of one of the greatest universities in the world, Charles Thomas Studd had it all. To top it off, he was good looking and full of charisma. Yet none of those things was his greatest asset. You see, as a believer in Jesus Christ, C. T. was more focused on the life to come than this one. That is rare for any person. It is especially rare for a young man with his wealth and stature.

When he graduated from Cambridge University, he gave up his sport, fame, fortune, and even his homeland, to become a missionary in China, India, and finally inland Africa. C. T. served Christ on the mission field from 1885 until his death in 1931.

Where is your treasure? What is your aim in life? A November 2013 study showed that there are over 199,235 people worldwide worth over $30 million in assets. Those 200,000 people are called "ultra high net worth people." Would your life be a success if you became "ultra high net worth"?

Early in our marriage my wife and I were invited to a Christian meeting. When we got there we met several other couples along with our friend and the speaker. The speaker asked what would make us really happy. One man raised his hand and said, "I'd really love to have a Porsche." So the speaker wrote "Porsche" on the board. A woman said, "I want to be a millionaire." So he wrote, "$1,000,000." Soon were added "Yacht," "Cruise around the world," and so forth.

Sharon and I sat there perplexed. While we wouldn't have minded any of those things, we knew that having them would not make us happy or fulfilled.

The Problem with Treasure on Earth

This problem of earthly treasure has plagued man throughout history. The pyramids contain the bodies of pharaohs who were buried with gold, diamonds, chariots, fine clothes, and even servants (who were buried alive!). Their idea was to take their treasure with them to the next life.[1]

However, earthly possessions are extremely perishable. The Lord Jesus put it this way,

> "Do not lay up for yourselves treasures on earth, where moth and rust destroy and where thieves break in and steal" (Matthew 6:19).

Though the Lord gives just three examples of the fleeting nature of treasures in this life, many more could be added. We've all had moths eat holes in our clothes. (I generally get about two years out of a running shirt before holes mysteriously appear.) Rust has eaten away at our possessions made of metal. (Recently the chassis of my lawn mower nearly disintegrated from rust.) Thieves have stolen from us. (My wife's purse and wedding ring were taken when we'd been married five years.)

The fence in our yard was decaying badly. A whole section was leaning. We had to replace it before it fell down. The fact is our earthly "treasures" steadily decay without constant repair.

The Beauty of Treasure in Heaven

Whereas earthly treasure decays, heavenly treasure is imperishable. The Lord went on to say,

> "But lay up for yourselves treasures in heaven, where neither moth nor rust destroys and where thieves do not break in and steal" (Matthew 6:20).

---

[1] It should be noted that even unbelievers in the ancient world believed in bodily resurrection. Clearly those who believed in the coming Messiah did as well, except they knew that the condition of being in the kingdom of the Messiah is faith in Him (Gen 15:6; John 8:56; Rom 4:1-5).

Treasure laid up in heaven is not subject to decay. Moths, rust, and thieves can't touch it. Neither can anything else. It is permanent.

Treasure we lay up in heaven is currently being reserved for us, to be given to us at the Judgment Seat of Christ for our use in the kingdom of God. While many think of this treasure as a figure of speech for some unspecified blessings, I see it as an eternal trust fund that believers will use to glorify God. The more we have stored up, the more we can give away in service to the Lord.

What? Who would need money in the kingdom? Well, no one, if the kingdom of God were going to be some ethereal experience, consisting of floating on clouds and strumming harps. However, the description of the eternal kingdom on the new earth in Revelation 21:24 strongly suggests the existence of an economy: "The kings of the earth [will] bring their glory and honor into it [the New Jerusalem]." Actually the majority of manuscripts read, "The kings of the earth [will] bring the glory and honor of the nations to Him."

In any case, the point is clear. The three wise men who brought gifts to the baby Jesus were types of rulers who, in the age to come, will forever bring gold and other treasures to the Lord Jesus.

Your Heart Is Where Your Treasure Is

The reason many believers aren't concerned with laying up treasure in heaven is because they're too preoccupied with laying it up here. They aren't aware that something much better exists. The Lord Jesus said,

> "For where your treasure is, there your heart will be also" (Matthew 6:21).

It is impossible to make it your aim to lay up treasure on this earth, and at the same time have your heart set on the things of God and the life to come.[2] What you value most is where your affections will be directed.

A few years ago, world-class athletes were asked the following question: "If you could take a drug that would cause you to win a gold medal, but it would kill you in ten years, would you take

---

[2] Just three verses later, the Lord Jesus made this point explicitly, saying: "No one can serve two masters; for either he will hate the one and love the other, or else he will be loyal to the one and despise the other. You cannot serve God and mammon [riches]" (Matthew 6:24).

it?" Amazingly, the majority said yes. They'd sacrifice fifty or more years of life for a gold medal.

What would you give up to have treasure in heaven? Would you drive a lesser car than you could otherwise afford? Live in a more modest home? Have a less expensive wardrobe? Enjoy simpler or fewer vacations? Give up fifty years of life (if called upon to be a martyr, for example)? The answer you give to these questions will depend on where your heart is.

Heavenly Treasure and Eternal Rewards

I talk a lot in this book about eternal rewards. Treasure reserved in heaven is just one of the many *types* of rewards that God will give. However, it differs from the other rewards in one major way: *it is guaranteed the moment it is laid up.* Every time you do a good deed with a proper motive, a deposit is made to your account in the Bank of Heaven (Matthew 10:42; Philippians 4:14-17). The more deposits you make, the more treasure you'll have with which to glorify God.

All other rewards will be given only to those who persevere in their service for Christ to the end of their lives. Those rewards include ruling with Christ, wearing white garments, the right to eat the hidden manna and the fruit of the tree of life, the right to enter the New Jerusalem by its gates, and a special name engraved on a beautiful white stone (Revelation 2:17; 3:4-5, 21; 22:14).[3]

There will be degrees of some or possibly all of these perseverance rewards. Some will rule, for example, over more cities than others (e.g., Luke 19:17, 19). But all who persevere will rule. The garments of some may shine more brightly than others (Matthew 17:2). But all who persevere will wear radiant garments.

Conclusion

At the age of twenty-five, C. T. Studd received a large inheritance. He chose to give away nearly the entire estate—an amount approaching $25 million in today's dollars.[4] Later, he and his wife Priscilla (Scilla) gave away the remainder of his inheritance.[5] C. T. and Priscilla believed what the Lord Jesus said. They were more

---

[3] For a discussion of Revelation 3:5, see my book *Confident in Christ* (Irving, TX: Grace Evangelical Society, 1999), 119-27.

[4] See www.jesusloversincleveland.org/English/biographies/studd/ctstudd.htm.

[5] Ibid. See also www.wholesomewords.org/missions/biostudd.html, p. 3.

concerned with laying up eternal treasure in heaven than having earthly treasure now.

Few of us have the fame and fortune of C. T. Studd. Still, all of us are tempted to live for the treasures this world has to offer. C. T. is famous for having said, "If Jesus Christ be God and died for me, then no sacrifice can be too great for me to make for Him." That is powerful stuff.

A proper view of treasure is an antidote to spiritual lethargy. Earthly treasure is guaranteed to perish. Treasure reserved for us in heaven will last forever. Focusing our affections on the riches of the life to come is a powerful way to energize our Christian lives. "For where your treasure is, there your heart will be also."

CHAPTER 10

Ruling with Christ

Estimates vary as to how many government employees the United States has. On the low end is a March 2013 U.S. Census Bureau report. It says that the U.S. has 19.6 million federal, state, and local employees.[1] Another estimate is 22.5 million.[2] Nearly one in five (17%) of U.S. workers are employed by the government.[3]

Additionally, according to the U.S. Census Bureau, there are over 27.7 million businesses in the U.S. That adds up to a lot more people in various levels of leadership.

One day the Lord Jesus is going to rule the entire world from the capital in Jerusalem. Many of His subjects will rule with Him. In the life to come, not all believers will have this opportunity. Only those who have earned that right will be in positions of authority.

A Lack of Ambition to Rule

I've met Christians who've told me that ruling with Christ just doesn't interest them. When pressed for a reason, their answers are usually vague. For the most part, they don't want to be in a position of authority over other people. Either they aren't supervisors at work (and don't want to be in the kingdom), or they are supervisors at work and don't like all the hassles involved in leading others.

---

[1] usgovinfo.about/b/2012/03/how-many-government-workers-does-it-take.htm.

[2] www.freerepublic.com/focus/news/2466363/posts.

[3] www.gallup.com/pull/141785/gov-employment-ranges-ohio.aspx.

Having a position of authority in this life is one thing. Ruling with Christ in the life to come is another.

Positions of authority in this life do give us a greater platform to glorify God. Consider, for example, the influence that stay-at-home moms have over their children. Training children to become godly adults is a huge responsibility that certainly glorifies God. However, any supervisory role in this life, even over one's children, is less than ideal, because both the supervisor and the ones being supervised are sinners. In the eternal kingdom there will be no sinners. Thus ruling with Christ will be far more satisfying and enjoyable, than supervising people in this life.

Co-Heirs with Christ

The idea of inheriting the kingdom and being a co-heir with Christ is one way the Bible speaks of ruling with Christ. We find this in a number of passages, as we shall now see.

All believers are children of God and hence heirs of God: "The Spirit Himself bears witness with our spirit that we are children of God, and if children, then heirs—heirs of God" (Romans 8:16-17a). However, not all believers will be co-heirs with Christ in the life to come. Only those who suffer with Him will earn the right to inherit the kingdom with Him. The passage just cited continues as follows: "...and joint heirs with Christ, if indeed we suffer with Him, that we may also be glorified together" (Romans 8:17b).

Believers are called to work heartily for the Lord that they may win the inheritance of ruling with Christ.

> And whatever you do, do it heartily, as to the Lord and not to men, knowing that from the Lord you will receive the reward of the inheritance; for you serve the Lord Christ. But he who does wrong will be repaid for the wrong which he has done, and there is no partiality (Colossians 3:23-25).

Paul presents two options for the believer. The believer who heartily serves God will receive the reward which is the inheritance of ruling with Christ. The believer who is unrighteous[4] in

---

[4] The Greek word translated "he who does wrong" is *adikōn*. It could be translated "the unrighteous." Not all believers live righteously. The same word is used in another inheritance passage, 1 Corinthians 6:9-11. There Paul says that the unrighteous—the

his behavior will not gain the inheritance, but will reap shame and rebuke instead.

Many other passages deal with the inheritance of ruling with Christ, or what I call *active inheritance*. The following are some to consider: Matthew 5:5; 19:29; 25:34; 1 Corinthians 6:9-11; 15:50; Galatians 5:19-21; Ephesians 5:5-7; Hebrews 1:14; 6:12; James 2:5; 1 Peter 1:4.[5]

I have a relative who was disinherited by her parents. She was still a member of the family and attended all of their gatherings. She was still much loved. But she was written out of the will. When the time came to inherit the assets of the parents, she received none.

So it is with some believers. All believers are members of the family of God. But only some will gain the inheritance of being co-heirs with Christ and ruling with Him in the life to come.

To Be His Partner

The Greek word *metochos* means *partner* or *partaker*. The term is used in a secular sense once in the New Testament to refer to Peter, James, and John, who, prior to following Jesus, had been *partners* in their fishing business (Luke 5:7).

All other New Testament uses of this term occur in Hebrews. Two of the five uses in Hebrews refer to being a "partaker" or "recipient" of the Holy Spirit (6:4) and of discipline (12:8). The remaining three refer to the potential future role of believers with Christ (1:9; 3:1, 14). We may be His *partners* in the life to come. Imagine what a glorious life that would be! But that potential will become a reality only if we hold fast our confession of hope until He returns (Hebrews 10:23-25).

Have you ever thought about being one of Jesus' *partners* in the life to come? As in any endeavor, partners work together. Thus

---

adikoi—will not inherit the kingdom of God. The main difference between the two passages is one uses the singular (*adikōn*) and the other the plural (*adikoi*).

[5] For more discussion of these passages see Joseph C. Dillow, *The Reign of the Servant Kings: A Study of Eternal Security and the Final Significance of Man* (Hayesville, NC: Schoettle Publishing Company, 1992), Zane C. Hodges, *Absolutely Free: A Biblical Reply to Lordship Salvation* (Corinth, TX: Grace Evangelical Society, 2014), *A Free Grace Primer* (Denton, TX: Grace Evangelical Society, 2011), and *The Epistle of James: Proven Character Through Testing* (Irving, TX: Grace Evangelical Society, 1994), Charles Stanley, *Eternal Security* (Nashville: Thomas Nelson Publishers, 1990), and my book, *Confident in Christ* (Irving, TX: Grace Evangelical Society, 1999).

partners of the King of kings are people who will share in His kingdom rule. They will not only be subjects in the kingdom, but they will also have special tasks to perform. They will have more authority and opportunity than others.

Believers who are partners of Christ will glorify Him more than those who are not. And as a result, their eternal experience will be more joyful (Hebrews 1:9).

To Sit on His Throne

Revelation 2–3 contains letters to seven churches. The penultimate verse in the seventh letter also serves to apply the message of all seven letters.

> "To him who overcomes I will grant to sit with Me on My throne, as I also overcame and sat down with My Father on His throne" (Revelation 3:21).

Sitting with the Lord on His throne is a figure for sharing in His kingdom rule.

The Reign of Servant Leaders

The Lord taught His disciples that those who rule in His kingdom will not lord it over their charges. Instead, they will be servant leaders.

> "The kings of the Gentiles exercise lordship over them, and those who exercise authority over them are called 'benefactors.' But not so among you; on the contrary, he who is greatest among you, let him be as the younger, and he who governs as he who serves…I am among you as the One who serves" (Luke 22:25-27).

The Lord illustrated this beautifully when He washed the feet of the disciples. After doing so He said, "For I have given you an example, that you should do as I have done to you…If you know these things, happy are you if you do them" (John 13:15, 17).

Jody Dillow's book *The Reign of the Servant Kings* captures this truth nicely. In Jesus' kingdom all rulers will be servant leaders. Rulership will not be arrogant domination, but humble direction, assistance, and service to others. Those who rule will delight in serving the Lord by serving His people and His program.

Rulers in the Life to Come

When I first became a Christian I had never heard of eternal rewards, and my concept of the kingdom was that we'd float on clouds and sing praise songs forever. Gradually I learned that our eternal destiny is not heaven, but the eternal kingdom that will be on the new earth (Revelation 21:1-3). Then I learned that we will do much more than sing, as glorious as that will be. We will serve Him forever (Revelation 22:3).

There is not room here to discuss in detail what the eternal kingdom will be like. I have, however, placed that discussion in Appendix C, "Whatever Happened to the New Earth? (Revelation 21-22)," in case you want to learn more.

To imagine what eternity will be like, we should start in the Garden of Eden. If Adam and Eve had not sinned, they would have fulfilled their mandate to be fruitful and multiply, fill the earth and subdue it, and have dominion over all of creation (Genesis 1:28). They would have built cities, roads, vehicles, farms, ranches, buildings, and so on. In other words, they would have developed a beautiful society that would have forever become more and more glorious.

God will still realize that vision, in spite of the Fall. First, He will establish a glorious kingdom on this earth during the Millennium. Then, after mankind's final rebellion, He will destroy this world and create the new heavens and the new earth (2 Peter 3:10-13; Revelation 21–22). That new creation will be flawless, with no taint of the Fall remaining.

On the new earth, we will realize the purpose for which we were created.

Rulership will be quite varied. Some will hold positions of authority in the new world government: Presidents, Governors, Mayors, City Council members, Judges, Legislators, and the like. Others will have authority within commerce. Surely the kingdom will have transportation companies, publishers, architectural firms, developers, utilities, entertainment and sports companies, and so on. All of these businesses will need people in various levels of management.

The more authority a person has, the more he or she will be able to glorify the Lord Jesus.

Conclusion

One of the great rewards available to believers is ruling with Christ; this is also called being co-heirs with Christ, or being His partners.

We are becoming now what we will be forever. We should live each day in light of the glorious prospect of ruling with Christ.

CHAPTER 11

Special Privileges

S pecial privileges motivate people to do their best by lightening their burdens and giving them more energy to do the job at hand. To have an office as opposed to a cubicle is a nice upgrade. Add a window to the office and things have improved even more. Your own washroom, and maybe your own elevator, puts you in the executive category.

But is it only in this life that special privileges exist? Or is it possible that the eternal rewards God gives include special privileges as well?

God-Honoring Clothing

The Lord Jesus promises that overcoming believers "shall walk with Me in white, for they are worthy" (Revelation 3:4).[1] Because some believers in this life overcome the world, they are worthy of honor. One of those honors is to wear special white garments.

Keep in mind that the Lord Jesus Himself will be clothed in dazzling white garments that will outshine all others. His glory will be supreme.

When at the Mount of Transfiguration He appeared in His glory, "His clothes became as white as the light" (Matthew 17:2). Special

---

[1] The next verse (Revelation 3:5) indicates that the Lord will not blot the name of the overcomer out of the Book of Life. That is an example of *litotes*, or understatement, because He won't blot anyone's name from the Book of Life. Rather, He is saying that He will pay tribute to the overcomer by giving him exalted garments and an exalted name.

clothing is not insignificant, because it honors a person. The more glorious the garments, the more honor to the wearer.

Like the sun, the Lord's garments will have maximum radiance. The garments of great servants like Moses, Elijah, Daniel, Deborah, Esther, and Mary will surely glow brightly. But theirs will be reflected glory, like the glory of the moon that reflects the glory of the sun.

Would you not want to be identified as closely as possible with the Lord Jesus and glorify Him, even in your clothing? The quality of your eternal garments will be determined by what you do in this life. Once this life is over, it will be too late to influence your worthiness to walk with Christ in white.

Life-Enhancing Foods

Food has multiple purposes in this life. Eating well increases one's energy and ability to function. In addition, food is one of life's pleasures. And, for the Christian in fellowship with God, the provision of food should increase our thankfulness to Him.

From the beginning God intended people to enjoy food. If Adam and Eve had not sinned, mankind would have forever eaten from the foods God provided. While many of us don't think of food in the life to come, we should.

At the Last Supper the Lord Jesus indicated He wouldn't drink of the fruit of the vine with His disciples again until He came in His kingdom. That means, of course, that He and they will enjoy drinking wine together in the kingdom.

After the Lord rose from the dead, He ate some fish and honey in the presence of His disciples (Luke 24:41-43). He also prepared fish for them and possibly shared that meal as well (John 21:9-15). Food will not be foreign to saints with glorified bodies. Surely all will eat, but some will enjoy special delicacies reserved only for persevering saints.

Two foods that will be reserved for believers who overcome in this life, are manna and the fruit of the tree of life.

The Lord said to the Church in Pergamos, "To him who overcomes I will give some of the hidden manna to eat" (Revelation 2:17). God fed Israel for forty years on manna (Exodus 16:15-16) and instructed them to put some away as a memorial to His provision. *Hidden manna* was that which was put away in the ark of the covenant (Hebrews 9:4). In eternity He will give manna to believers who overcame in this life.

This manna will surely provide the benefits good food offers today: increased energy, enhanced ability to serve God, and enjoyment. Eating that bread will forever remind us that the Lord Jesus is the Bread of Life (see John 6:35).

The Church at Ephesus heard this promise, "To him who overcomes I will give to eat from the tree of life, which is in the midst of the Paradise of God" (Revelation 2:7; see also 22:14). The tree of life was in the original Paradise, the Garden of Eden. It would have granted fullness of life to mankind if the Fall had not occurred. But if fallen men had eaten of it, they would have lived forever in unglorified bodies. So Adam and Eve were banished from the Garden. But the tree will flourish in the kingdom, providing a different fruit each month (Revelation 22:2), and enhancing the lives of those who eat of it. This special privilege is available only for believers who persevere.

Special Entrance

When my friend Al visited the Middle East, an Israeli tour guide told him about a VIP entrance into a Middle Eastern city which only special dignitaries were permitted to use. The New Jerusalem will have twelve such entrances.

It is quite probable that there will be more ways to enter the New Jerusalem than through its twelve gates of pearl. While all believers will be able to enter the city, only select believers will enter by the gates. "Blessed are those who do His commandments, that they may...enter through the gates into the city" (Revelation 22:14).

In the Old Testament to be "in the gates" was a privilege reserved for the elders of the city. Citizens would come there to ask the elders for their judgment in matters (see Ruth 4:9-10).

To enter the New Jerusalem through one of its twelve gates will be a great honor reserved only for those believers who overcame in this life.

A New Name

To have a good name is always important, and is especially so in the Bible. When God changed the names of people, their new names were significant. Jacob became Israel, Prince with God (Genesis 32:28). Simon became Peter, the Rock (Matthew 16:18).

A white stone engraved with a unique name will be given to every overcomer.

> "And I will give him a white stone, and on the stone a new name written which no one knows except him who receives it" (Revelation 2:17).

Imagine the joy of having a stone engraved with the Lord's special name for you!

One motivation to hang in there when things get tough now is to realize that our new name hangs in the balance.

Fullness of Life

The Lord Jesus said that He came that we might have life, and that we might have it more abundantly (John 10:10). All believers have eternal life now, but not all have the same abundance of that life. One who has walked with Christ for decades surely is experiencing a more abundant life than one who has walked with Him for a few days.

How much glory, honor, and authority we will have in the life to come is directly related to what we have done with our Christian lives. The more we do for Christ in this life, assuming our motives are right (see Matthew 6:1-21), the more abundant our eternal experience will be.

These Privileges Benefit Everyone

We must not think that these privileges are solely for the benefit of the recipient. We have been made to glorify God by loving and serving others. These privileges will enable overcomers to do just that. Thus everyone benefits and the Lord Himself will be pleased.

Conclusion

If the Lord wants you to have these privileges of a lifetime well spent, then it is a false spirituality that says, "Oh, I don't want any special privileges." You will, if you want for yourself what the Lord obviously desires for all His children.

CHAPTER 12

His Approval

My father died when I was thirty-seven. How I had longed for his approval, wanting him to be pleased with me and with what I had done with my life.

Sadly, that was not to be. My dad's father was an alcoholic and a perfectionist. My dad could never do enough to gain his father's approval. When he became a man and started his own family, he continued that legacy with my sisters and me.

Don't get me wrong. My dad loved me very much and made that clear, and yet he just couldn't approve of me. He accepted me, but his approval never came.

After my dad died in 1989, I found myself searching for others who would approve of me. Many men reminded me of my dad. But guess what—*they didn't approve of me either.*

One day I realized that the approval I was longing for is not from men, but from God. I want to hear the Lord Jesus say, "Well done, good servant" (Luke 19:17).

Many Christians fail to realize that it is possible to obtain God's approval. But, once they grasp this truth, it becomes a powerful force in their lives.

Aiming for God's Approval

Paul's aim in life was to gain the Lord's approval:

> But I discipline my body and bring it into subjection, lest, when I have preached to others, I myself should become disqualified [disapproved] (1 Corinthians 9:27).

The Greek word translated "disqualified" is *adokimos.* The addition of the letter "a" before a word in Greek often negates it. We find the same thing in English. For example, the opposite of a *theist* is an *atheist.*

The word *dokimos* means "approved." For example, in 2 Timothy 2:15, the verse made famous by AWANA, Paul urged Timothy to be diligent to show himself an "approved" (*dokimos*) workman who need not be ashamed. Disapproved (*adokimos*) workmen will indeed be ashamed of themselves before Christ (compare 1 John 2:28).

You may wonder, what's the difference? If I'm sure I'm saved, then God approves of me, right? Wrong. Approval and acceptance are two different things in Scripture. Paul makes that clear in 1 Corinthians 9:24-27. He knew he had eternal life and was accepted by the Lord. But he was not sure he would persevere in the faith and maintain the Lord's approval.

God *accepts* all who have come to faith in Christ, no matter how they are living, or whether they are serving Him. Whether they pray, read the Word, or go to church. To have eternal life we must simply believe in Christ for it (John 6:47). However, to gain His *approval*, we must do more than believe in Christ (1 Corinthians 9:24-27).

If you are a good parent, you always *accept* your children. But does that mean you always *approve* of them? Of course not! What if one of your children were arrested for selling cocaine? You would still accept him, but you would *not* approve of him.

The Good Housekeeping Seal of Approval means that the Good Housekeeping Institute has evaluated a particular product and concluded that its quality is worthy of endorsement. So it is with God. If the Lord approves of you, He considers you a good servant; He commends you for what you are doing for Him.

What Approval Will Mean

Even if no additional privileges and rulership were available, His approval alone would be wonderful. Imagine going through eternity knowing that the Lord approved of you. You would forever delight in the memory of the day He told you, "Well done, good and faithful servant" (Luke 19:17).

Of course, approval will grant one a special status in the kingdom. The approved will be a group of saints distinguished by their clothing, diet, and other privileges.

If you grew up in a functional home and received your dad's approval, you know this impacts every day of your life. It is part of who you are. If, like me, you grew up without it, that too is part of who you are. You can overcome it, of course, by developing your identity in Christ.

If you are walking in fellowship with Him, then currently you are approved by Him (e.g., Romans 16:10). If you maintain fellowship with Him, you will forever be one of the approved.

I can't stress enough how important it is that you live each day in light of eternity. He has given us all we need to gain His approval. The Holy Spirit lives within each believer and enables us to be godly persons (2 Peter 1:3), but it is *not* automatic. We must live by faith in Christ (Galatians 2:20), allowing God to transform our lives by the renewing of our minds (Romans 12:1-2; 2 Corinthians 3:18; Ephesians 4:23).

Confidence or Shame?

Those are our options when we appear before the Lord Jesus at His Judgment Seat. The Apostle John put it this way:

> And now, little children, abide in Him, that when He appears, we may have confidence and not be ashamed before Him at His coming (1 John 2:28).

Certainly any shame the glorified saint experiences will be short-lived. However, what should be a glorious day of honor can in reality be a day of regret (compare 1 John 4:17-19; see also Chapter 5).

It is equally certain that the approved believer will forever have a special measure of confidence and joy.

Oh, how I want His approval.

CHAPTER 13

Fullness Forever

When I was a child, I didn't have much patience for delayed gratification. A reward that was more than a day off motivated me little, if at all. As I matured I learned to delay gratification, and came to be highly motivated by rewards that were years away.

I planned on spending seven to eight years in seminary to get both my master's and doctoral degrees. That is a long time for a young man. Yet I hung in there because I was convinced that the degrees would have a positive impact on the rest of my life. Seven years of preparation was a small price to pay for an enhanced ability to understand, apply, and teach God's Word.

Businesses use various incentives to motivate people to do their best work. For people in sales, there are three types of prizes: cash, merchandise, and trips. Top managers are given cash bonuses as well as promotions, increased base salaries, and stock options.

Christianity offers incentives too. One of these is eternal reward. Although there are rewards now for the believer, most of them won't be given to us until after this life is over and we appear before the Judgment Seat of Christ. This may mean waiting decades to receive them.

Thus, the length of time these rewards will last once we receive them, makes a difference as to how motivated we will be to obtain them and how meaningful they will be to us once we do. Of those who believe in eternal rewards as an idea distinct from eternal salvation, there are three views concerning how long rewards last: a few minutes, a thousand years, or forever.

A Few Minutes?

Revelation 4:10-11 states,

> ...the twenty-four elders fall down before Him who sits on the throne and worship Him who lives forever and ever, *and cast their crowns before the throne*, saying: "You are worthy, O Lord, To receive glory and honor and power; For You created all things, And by Your will they exist and were created" (italics added).

Some Bible students are highly influenced by this passage, believing it to mean that all rewards given to believers by Christ will be returned to Him immediately after the Bema.[1]

In the first place, they argue that verse 10 says that, "the twenty-four elders...cast their crowns before the throne." Since crowns represent a type of eternal reward, the casting of crowns at Jesus' feet suggests to some that we will give our rewards back to Him immediately after receiving them.

In the second place, it is felt that verse 11 indicates that the casting down of crowns shows that all glory, honor, and power belong to the Lord Jesus. If we were to retain eternal rewards, we would be robbing the Lord of the glory, honor, and power that are uniquely His.

While on the surface these arguments might sound convincing, they really hold about as much water as a colander.

Concerning the casting down of crowns, most people forget that verse 10 is actually the middle of a sentence that begins at verse 9:

> *Whenever* the living creatures give glory and honor and thanks to Him who sits on the throne, who lives forever and ever, the twenty-four elders fall down...and cast their crowns...(emphasis mine).

---

[1] One might legitimately wonder how a reward held for only a few minutes is truly a reward. Some of those holding this view respond by saying that while the rewards are ours for only a few minutes, we have eternal satisfaction and joy in knowing that we gave our crowns back to the Lord. Yet there is no text which says this. Additionally, as we shall see, there are many texts which directly indicate that we retain forever the rewards we receive.

Notice the word *whenever* in verse 9. The crown-casting in verse 10 is not a one-time event. It is repeated again and again. Indeed, *every* time the living creatures say, "Holy, holy, holy, Lord God Almighty, who was and is and is to come!" (verse 8b), then the twenty-four elders cast down their crowns. And according to the first half of verse 8, the living creatures "do not rest day or night…"

This crown-casting clearly does not refer to something believers are doing after the Judgment Seat of Christ. This is an ongoing event in which a small number of beings (angelic beings, in light of Revelation 7:11) participate.

While all glory, honor, and power come from the Lord Jesus, this in no way suggests He will not share these with others. Indeed, He promised to share these blessings with believers who persevere (compare Matthew 16:27; 2 Timothy 2:12; Hebrews 1:9; 1 Peter 4:13; Revelation 2:26; 3:21). Allowing humans to have some measure of glory, honor, and power in no way diminishes Christ's glory. If it did, Moses' face would never have shone. Elijah wouldn't have been taken up to heaven in a whirlwind and flaming chariot. David would never have been king of Israel. The Lord Jesus would not be called the Son of David. He would not have promised the Apostles that they would rule over the twelve tribes of Israel. He wouldn't have given Adam and Eve and all of mankind dominion over the earth. And so on.

This view has nothing substantial to commend it. The only passage used to prove it fails to do so. Furthermore, other passages make it clear that rewards are lasting.

One Thousand Years?

Influenced by Revelation 20:4-6, others are convinced that rewards will last only as long as the Millennium.

> And I saw thrones, and they sat on them, and judgment was committed to them. Then I saw the souls of those who had been beheaded for their witness to Jesus and for the word of God, who had not worshiped the beast or his image, and had not received his mark on their foreheads or on their hands. And they lived and reigned with Christ for a thousand years. But the rest of the dead did not live again until the thousand years were finished. This is the

first resurrection. Blessed and holy is he who has part in the first resurrection. Over such the second death has no power, but they shall be priests of God and of Christ, and shall reign with Him a thousand years.

Twice in these verses we see that saints who were martyred during the Tribulation will rule with Christ for a thousand years. Many view this as concrete evidence that rewards will cease after the Millennium.

The problem with this view is that no verses can be cited, including Revelation 20:4-6, that *limit* rulership and the other rewards to the Millennium. While it is true that the rewards will be enjoyed *during* the Millennium, it is not necessarily true that they will end when it does.

Forever?

If even one passage made it clear that rewards are unending, the issue would be settled. The fact is we have not one, but many.

When Paul speaks of the prize, or crown, we are seeking, he says that it is *imperishable* (1 Corinthians 9:25), contrasting it with a *perishable* crown. If our rewards lasted for one thousand years, they would be *perishable*. Remember, with the Lord a thousand years is as but a single day. Yet Paul says this will be an *imperishable* crown. An *imperishable* crown is an eternal one![2]

The Lord Jesus commands us to lay up treasure in heaven (Matthew 6:19-21), where moths and rust can never destroy it, nor thieves steal it. Clearly these are descriptions intended to convey *permanence*.

Peter spoke of an imperishable and undefiled inheritance in 1 Peter 1:4. While most commentators take this verse to refer to eternal salvation, the context actually supports the view that the author had the matter of eternal rewards in mind.

---

[2] Of course, some might say that the crowns themselves are imperishable, yet we do not retain them. If we give them back to the Lord Jesus, He can keep them forever. However, the context of 1 Corinthians 9:24-27 does not support that possibility. Clearly Paul is thinking of a crown we retain forever. "Run in such a way that you may obtain it" (verse 24). If the crown were imperishable, but we would only keep it for a few minutes, his whole argument collapses. In that case the athlete who received the perishable crown actually enjoyed it longer than the believer who "obtained" an imperishable crown.

In 1977 I spent a week with Josh McDowell while he spoke at Marshall University. At that time I thought 1 Peter 1:4 was a statement about eternal security. I'll never forget Josh's reply when I mentioned it. He said, "Yes, but those who reject eternal security will point out that Peter says that this inheritance is 'kept by the power of God *through faith...*' They will reply that ongoing faith is required."[3]

I've come to see that Josh's hypothetical objection is legitimate. Peter was not thinking of the initial faith by which one gains eternal life, nor was he making a point about eternal security. Rather, he was talking about the fact that the rewards that the Lord will give at the Bema will be eternal.

The readers, who were believers (1:2, 23; 2:7), were experiencing persecution (verse 6). Their faith would pass the test only if they persevered (verse 7). In that case they would gain "praise, honor, and glory at the revelation of Jesus Christ" (verse 7).[4]

In the Book of Revelation, it is clear that Christ's rewards will extend beyond the Millennium into the eternal kingdom. Revelation 21:24 speaks of the kings of the earth in the eternal kingdom. In Revelation 22:12 the Lord Jesus says:

> "And behold, I am coming quickly, and My reward is with Me, to give to every one according to his work."

Overcoming Christians are then promised that they will be rewarded with "the right to the tree of life" (22:14a). They will also be permitted to enter the New Jerusalem by its twelve gates (22:14b). The tree of life and the New Jerusalem won't even *be* on earth until after the Millennium and the destruction of the current heavens and earth (compare Revelation 21:1-3).

---

[3] The verse contained in this quote goes on to say, "for salvation ready to be revealed in the last time" (1 Peter 1:5). That salvation is spoken of again a few verses later, "receiving the end of your faith—the salvation of your souls" (verse 9). The saving of the soul is often used in Scripture to refer to physical deliverance from death. Compare 1 Peter 3:20 concerning the salvation of eight souls via Noah's ark. However, here it is clearly an eschatological salvation: "reserved in heaven...ready to be revealed in the last time." This salvation of the souls or lives of believers parallels Matthew 16:24-28 that also deals with eschatological salvation. (See Chapter 7.) Only those believers who persevere in faith and good works will rule with Christ in the life to come.

[4] See Joseph C. Dillow, *The Reign of the Servant Kings: A Study of Eternal Security and the Final Significance of Man* (Hayesville, NC: Schoettle Publishing Company, 1992), 572.

Ultimate Prizes

Imagine if God guaranteed you $100 million here and now if you persevered in faith and good works for twenty years. I think the number desiring to serve the Lord would go up significantly.

Well, what if God offered something better than that? A person who received $100 million at age forty would have only a few decades to enjoy it. What if God offered rewards that last forever, not just for a few decades? Wouldn't that be far superior?

Ruling with Christ forever is priceless. The hidden manna and the fruits from the tree of life will be wonderful blessings. Treasure that is currently being stored up for us in heaven is something we will enjoy forever.

Many Christians place more hope on winning the lottery than they do on gaining meaningful eternal rewards. Either they are completely unaware of what God says, or they are convinced the rewards won't be that special.

Mary Decker Slaney is arguably the greatest female athlete the U.S. has ever produced, setting twenty-six U.S. and seventeen world records during her amazing career. In 1982 she was the top female runner in the world in all distances from 800 meters to 10,000 meters (one-half mile up to six miles). Due to an injury, she missed the 1976 Olympics. She missed the 1980 Olympics in Russia because of the U.S. boycott of the games. Favored to win the gold in both the 1,500 and 3,000 meters in the 1984 Los Angeles Olympics, Mary decided to compete only in the 3,000 meter race in order to reduce the risk of injury. In the finals of the 3,000 she was in the lead, running strong, and it appeared she would easily win the race. Then Zola Budd, a barefoot runner from South Africa, with little international experience, accidentally tripped Mary. Down to the track she went. As she was writhing in pain in the infield, the race went on without her.

Mary competed in the 1988 and 1996 Olympics, but failed to win any medals. During her career she underwent twenty leg, foot, and ankle operations in order to keep her running career alive. Imagine all the pain of the surgeries and recoveries. And anyone who has run track knows that the workouts are very painful, even for a healthy runner.

Mary had a drive within her that was intense. Her motivations were likely numerous: a love for running competitively, a desire for fame and fortune, the lure of the medals and the cheering crowds, and traveling around the world. For over twenty years she experienced these things.

The Apostles were that intense in their service for Christ. And so should we all be. Our motivations are numerous as well: present blessings, avoiding God's discipline, gratitude, joy of service, a desire to please and glorify God, as well as a desire to gain eternal rewards.

Eternal rewards are eternal. They are the ultimate in delayed gratification. God guarantees it.

Section 4
How Should This Impact My Life Now?

"Therefore I run thus:
not with uncertainty.
Thus I fight:
not as one who beats the air.
But I discipline my body
and bring it into subjection,
lest, when I have preached to others,
I myself should become disqualified."

1 Corinthians 9:26-27

CHAPTER 14

Prepare to Meet the Judge (James 5:9)

Courtroom shows are fascinating. Why? They involve real-life drama that we can all relate to. As the evidence comes in, we form our own opinions of innocence or guilt and wonder how the judge will rule. A range of emotion washes over us: thankfulness for what we have, anger at unrepentant evil, a desire for justice, identification with the plaintiff or defendant, respect for the judge, as well as satisfaction in what we perceive is a fair verdict. No one viewing these shows would envy the role of a defendant clearly at fault. We wouldn't want our shortcomings to be revealed and judged!

I have appeared in court twice—for traffic violations. As a teenager I was ticketed for speeding and I went to court to try to avoid a fine. I stood before a judge, confessed my guilt, and apologized for breaking the law.

My second run-in with the law occurred in 1974, just days after the speed limit was reduced from 65 to 55. A graduate student at the time, I was driving to my teaching assistant job at a local junior college. The officer clocked me at 60, but my speedometer read 55. I thought I had kept to the speed limit. I had even seen the highway patrolman in my mirror. I decided to fight the ticket in court—and lost. The judge informed me that the patrol car speedometers are checked each month. "Yours is off," he said bluntly. "Get it fixed."

Like the police, we need to check our standards regularly. We may think that we are good judges of what is right and wrong, but if our standards disagree with those set forth in the Word of God, we are wrong. Like it or not, the Bible makes it clear that *every* person will have his or her day in court—unbelievers after the Millennium at the Great White Throne Judgment,[1] and believers before the Millennium at the Judgment Seat of Christ.[2]

The Judge Is Coming

We often speak of the Lord Jesus Christ as our *Savior*. But when is the last time you heard Him referred to as our *Judge*? Can't remember? Why is that? Maybe it's because it's sobering to think that we as believers are accountable for our actions. Whether we realize it or not, our Savior is returning someday as our Judge.

Many believers wrongly assume that because they have eternal life, they won't be judged for the things they have done as Christians. After all, if all their sin is covered under the blood of Christ, why does it matter how they live?[3] They might give lip service to living for Christ, but many Christians feel that if they are lax in their service, it won't really matter.

James, the half-brother of the Lord Jesus, was under no such illusion, having heard Jesus teach on this topic many times. He knew that all believers will be judged—but not to determine our eternal destiny, for Jesus promised we wouldn't come into judgment for that (John 5:24).[4] Yet there will be a time when all the words and deeds of Christians will be examined. James wrote:

---

[1] It is possible that believers will be observers or even witnesses at the trial of the unsaved. Revelation 20:11-15 discusses the Great White Throne Judgment.

[2] The Bible is not clearer than that on the time of the Bema. It could occur during the Tribulation or during the 75 days between the end of the Tribulation and the start of the Millennium (Daniel 12:11-12). In any case, we will surely experience time differently during the Bema than we do now, for if believers are judged one at a time (which Luke 19:11-26 suggests), each judgment will last only a fraction of a second.

[3] If the blood of Christ covers all our sins, how could the Lord consider any of our bad deeds? See Chapter 5, p. 36, for an answer to that question.

[4] Scripture doesn't contradict itself. The obvious way to harmonize texts that say believers will and won't be judged is to realize that two different types of judgment are in view. The context of John 5:24 is eternal salvation: "He who hears My word and believes in Him who sent Me has everlasting life, and shall not come into judgment, but has passed from death into life." The point is that those who have eternal life will not be judged at the Great White Throne Judgment (Revelation 20:11-15). Their eternal destiny is already set (compare John 3:18 and the present tense, "is not condemned"). However, believers will be judged *at the Judgment Seat of Christ* (compare Romans 14:10-12 and 2 Corinthians 5:9-10). The purpose of that judgment is to determine degrees of reward, not eternal destiny.

Do not grumble against one another, brethren, lest you be condemned. Behold, the Judge is standing at the door! (James 5:9).

Grumbling against others is a problem for me. Even after thirty years as a believer, I still struggle with this, as do many Christians. Imagine standing before the Lord Jesus and having Him evaluate all you have said and done since you came to faith in Him for eternal life. There are a lot of things I've said and done that I'd just as soon the Judge not consider.

Isn't that the point James is making? We should live today in light of the fact that the Judge is at the door and ready to judge us for all we say and do. In his commentary on James, Zane Hodges states:

> This sense of the imminency of the Savior's return is captured in the striking metaphor, *Behold, the Judge is standing at the door.* Like a Roman lictor announcing a judge's impending entry, as it were, James cries, "Quiet!" His Christian readers must fully silence their complaints against one another in the realization that their Lord and Judge can at any moment appear and sit down on the Bema (Judgment Seat) in order to assess their lives...They must therefore be careful that He does not find them nurturing a complaining spirit against their fellow believers. As Paul has so clearly stated, *So then each of us shall give account of himself to God. Therefore let us not judge one another anymore* (Rom 14:12-13a).[5]

There is great power in the following truths:

• Jesus could return for believers at any moment.

• When He comes, we will be judged. We can't hide from His judgment; He sees all.

• Our options are shame or confidence before our Lord (1 John 2:28).

• Only believers who are persevering in faith and good works will rule with Christ forever (e.g., 2 Timothy 2:12).

---

[5] Zane C. Hodges, *The Epistle of James: Proven Character Through Testing* (Irving, TX: Grace Evangelical Society, 1994), 111-12, emphasis his.

• The Lord Jesus is not only our Savior—He is also our Judge!

The Motivation for Endurance

In December 1998, I completed the Dallas White Rock Marathon in five hours and twenty-seven minutes, racewalking rather than running because of knee and hip injuries. But I endured because I wanted to receive the finishers's medal. More than that, I wanted what that medal represented. I hung in there through a tough race. All the hours spent in training over the previous eighteen months had paid off. That was a great feeling of accomplishment.

But as good as it was, it doesn't hold a candle to the approval and praise of the Lord Jesus Christ that awaits the believer who finishes the race of life faithfully serving his Savior.

Would I have finished that marathon within the six-hour time limit had I not trained for it? I don't think so. Twenty-six miles is a long way! Knowing that the day was coming motivated me to train to be ready for the challenge.

The reality of the coming Judgment Seat of Christ (the Bema) provides a powerful motivation to endure. That is why it is so sad that the vast majority of people sitting in churches every Sunday know little or nothing about the Bema.

It's vital for us as Christians to know that we are accountable. Someday the Lord Jesus will return. And when He does, He will judge us for what we have done during our Christian lives. To borrow a phrase from Dr. Earl Radmacher, "This life is training time for reigning time." How true.

CHAPTER 15

Remember Your Inheritance
(Galatians 5:19-21)

On April 9, 1994, Marie S. Georgeoff died at the age of ninety, leaving one-third of her estate to each of her surviving sons, Edward and Donald, and the children of her deceased son, Thomas. According to the January 3, 2001 issue of the *Akron Beacon Journal,* Donald, the executor of the estate, claimed that his mother's estate was worth only $6,500, the value of a vacant lot she owned.

Thomas's children filed suit, alleging that the estate was worth well over $1 million, nearly all of it in cash. The children remembered that their grandparents, who had made a fortune with a restaurant, bar, and gambling parlor in Akron, kept boxes of cash in their home.

It made a big difference to Thomas's children whether they split one-third of $6,500 or one-third of a million dollars. They were convinced that Donald and his family were hiding their grandmother's money.

We have all heard stories like this, where one relative allegedly takes most of the inheritance, in violation of the will.

While no one can take away our God-given inheritance, we *can* forfeit it by the way we live. How much we will receive depends on how we live our Christian lives. To receive the ultimate inheritance—ruling with Christ—we must persevere in faith and good works.

On three occasions the Apostle Paul listed various vices, warning that people who live like that "will not inherit the kingdom of God" (1 Corinthians 6:9-11; Galatians 5:19-21; and Ephesians 5:5-7). I have chosen Galatians 5:19-21 as the representative text:

> Now the works of the flesh are evident, which are: adultery, fornication, uncleanness, licentiousness, idolatry, sorcery, hatred, contentions, jealousies, outbursts of wrath, selfish ambitions, dissensions, heresies, envy, murders, drunkenness, revelries, and the like; of which I tell you beforehand, just as I also told you in time past, that those who practice such things will not inherit the kingdom of God.

What's Going on Here?

Could this be the same Apostle Paul who wrote, "By grace you have been saved through faith, and that not of yourselves; it is the gift of God, not of works, lest anyone should boast" (Ephesians 2:8-9)? And also, "Not by works of righteousness which we have done, but according to His mercy He saved us" (Titus 3:5)? And again, "Now to him who works, the wages are not counted as grace but as debt. But to him who does not work but believes on Him who justifies the ungodly, his faith is accounted for righteousness" (Romans 4:4-5)?

Recognizing the tension here, commentators find various ways to harmonize these passages. Let's examine a few.

Good Works Required to Stay Saved

Those who believe that eternal life can be lost argue that while *initial* salvation is by grace through faith, *final* salvation requires ongoing good works. In other words, the gift is taken back if the recipient doesn't remain worthy of it.

This view is not a harmonization at all because it contradicts the many places in which Paul speaks of justification as apart from works. Paul is not referring merely to pre-salvation works, but to works, period. Notice that if any works are the cause of our salvation, then we have grounds for boasting, and God is indebted to us. Yet Paul says that conclusion cannot be true.

Good Works Required to Prove One Is Saved

Another effort at solving this dilemma comes from Reformed theology, which suggests that all *true* Christians persevere in faith and good works. Thus no *genuine* believer could die as an immoral man, an alcoholic, or even as a jealous or angry man, since those character traits are on the vice lists as well.

The problem with this view is that it still makes good works a condition of getting into the kingdom and fails to harmonize the passages. If you got into the kingdom because you persevered in good works, and another person didn't because he failed to, you would have grounds for boasting and God would be your debtor.

Of course, Reformed theology has an answer for this. It says that it is God who accomplishes the works. Thus they are really *His* works, not *our* works. This sounds good. Yet when asked why there is a passage like this one that, in their opinion, threatens believers with hell, their response is that God uses the threats to motivate us to strive to do good works.

Say what? If they are God's works, then *He* does them. We wouldn't need to cooperate at all. There would be no striving, no need of threats. God is surely powerful enough to make sure we persevere, if that is what He guarantees we will do.

However, God doesn't do this. Unless the believer cooperates with the work of the Holy Spirit, perseverance will not occur.

Besides, there really is no difference between losing your salvation and proving you weren't saved in the first place. You end up in hell either way. Both views make perseverance in good works a requirement of getting into the kingdom—which directly contradicts Paul elsewhere in Scripture.

Assurance is based solely on the promises of the Lord that all who simply believe in Him have everlasting life. No strings attached.

Good Works Required for Inheritance

Here is a simple solution that harmonizes the passages. *Entrance* into the kingdom is attained by grace through faith, apart from works. Yet Paul is warning believers that they will not *inherit* the kingdom if they indulge in wickedness. *Entrance* and *inheritance* are two separate issues.

The Scriptures speak of two types of inheritance for the believer. The first is what I call *passive inheritance*. All believers inherit many things simply because they are children of God.

Second is what I call *active inheritance*. Only those believers who persevere in faith and good works will inherit these things: rulership with Christ, His approval, and the right to wear special white garments, to mention just a few.

In Galatians 5:19-21, *inheriting the kingdom* refers to *active inheritance*. Compare 1 Corinthians 9:24-27, where Paul fears he would not be approved. Or 2 Timothy 2:12, where he warns that only those who endure will reign with Christ. Or Galatians 6:7-9, where he says that only those who sow to the Spirit will reap a full experience of eternal life.

One passage in which both types of inheritance can be easily seen together is Romans 8:16-17. It reads:

> The Spirit Himself bears witness with our spirit that we are children of God, and if children, then heirs—heirs of God and joint heirs with Christ, if indeed we suffer with Him, that we may also be glorified together.

All believers are passive heirs because they are children of God. There are things that they have now and will have forever, no matter what they do. These include four ministries of the Holy Spirit which occur at the moment we first believe in Christ for eternal life. I remember these ministries with the acronym RIBS. The Spirit regenerates, indwells, baptizes (into the Body of Christ), and seals us the moment we believe in Jesus.

Other aspects of passive inheritance are citizenship in God's kingdom and future resurrection with glorified bodies. None of these things are dependent on our perseverance. They are thus things we *passively* inherit.

However, there is a type of inheritance that is limited to those believers who persevere in their service for Christ. Those believers who live for Christ and hence "suffer with Him" will be "joint heirs with Christ" and will also be "glorified together" with Him. This co-heirship and co-glorification includes ruling with Christ forever. Only those believers who persevere in self-sacrificing service for Christ will receive this active type of inheritance.

Don't forget about your inheritance. While you can't lose eternal life, you *can* fail to inherit the kingdom. Like the Prodigal Son, as long as we are in the spiritual far country, we are not in fellowship with the Father and we have squandered our inheritance. Willful rebellion against the Lord will result in forfeiture of the right to reign with Christ. Only when we return to fellowship with Him can we once again be in line to inherit.

CHAPTER 16

Walk Without Stumbling (Jude 24)

One of the greatest fears many churchgoers have is that they will fall away from the Lord and either lose their salvation or prove that they weren't really saved in the first place.

The net effect of these two fears is the same: A lack of assurance that is terrifying. What an awful way to go through life.

We should fear falling away from the Lord—not because we will end up in hell, for believers are eternally secure (John 11:26)—but because our fullness of life in eternity is directly related to our perseverance in the faith now.

Jude 24 concerns the problem of falling away and its associated loss of joy. As he closes his epistle, Jude writes:

> Now to Him who is able to keep you from stumbling, And to present you faultless Before the presence of His glory with exceeding joy... (Jude 24).

God is able to keep every believer from stumbling, that is, from experiencing major moral or doctrinal failure. A key question here is whether Jude was conveying *an unconditional guarantee* that God will keep all believers from stumbling or whether he was referring to *a conditional guarantee* that requires a certain response by believers.

Both in light of Scripture and experience, the idea that this is an unconditional guarantee is impossible. We need only to think of saints like David, Solomon, Peter, John Mark, and Demas—all of whom stumbled badly.

Nevertheless, a number of pastors and theologians suggest that Jude 24 *is* an unconditional promise.[1] One author uses Jude 24 in an effort to prove his contention that, "God *will* keep His own [from apostasy]."[2]Another cites Jude 24 as proof "of the perseverance of God in protecting and preserving His people in faith."[3]

I believe that many commentators have missed the mark in explaining this text. Jude 24 *calls* for perseverance, but does not *guarantee* it. Furthermore, it is not dealing with eternal security at all.

Ability Is Not a Guarantee

Nothing bad that happens is outside of God's control. Take, for example, the Fall of Adam and Eve. God could have created our first parents without the ability to sin, but He didn't. He could have kept the serpent from tempting them, but He didn't.

Consider three examples where the expressions *God is able*, *He is able*, and *I am able* (where Jesus is the speaker) are used. In each, the possible result either never occurred or it occurred only when a condition was met.

(1) John the Baptist said, "*God is able* to raise up children to Abraham from these stones" (Matthew 3:9, emphasis mine). He was able to do that, but He never did.

(2) The author of Hebrews wrote, "*He is able* to aid those who are tempted" (Hebrews 2:18, emphasis mine). While God is able to aid those who are tempted, the author of Hebrews indicates that this aid is conditioned upon the one being tempted looking to Him in prayer with faith (Hebrews 3:12-15; 4:11-16). Hebrews 2:18 is in no

---

[1] See, for example, Edward C. Pentecost, "Jude," in *The Bible Knowledge Commentary*, New Testament edition (Wheaton, IL: Victor Books, 1983), 2:923-24; Edwin A. Blum, "Jude," in the *Zondervan NIV Bible Commentary*, Vol. 2, New Testament (Grand Rapids, MI: Zondervan Publishing House, 1994), 1124; Michael Green, *The Second Epistle of Peter and the Epistle of Jude*, Tyndale New Testament Commentaries (Grand Rapids, MI: Wm. B. Eerdmans Publishing Company, 1968), 189-91. Also see notes 2 and 3 below.

[2] John F. MacArthur, Jr., *The Gospel According to Jesus: What Is Authentic Faith?*, revised and expanded anniversary edition (Grand Rapids, MI: Zondervan Publishing House, 2008), 109. See also n. 7 on page 109 where he says that 2 Timothy 2:19 "underscores the truth that saving faith, which is wrought by God, cannot fail. We cannot always see whose faith is genuine and whose is a sham, but God knows."

[3] Donald S. Whitney, *How Can I Be Sure I'm a Christian?: What the Bible Says About Assurance of Salvation* (Colorado Springs, CO: NavPress Publishing Group, 1994), 29.

way a blanket promise that God will aid all who are tempted. The Christian who is away from God and who isn't praying for God's help will find that he is unable, in his own strength, to successfully meet the challenges of the temptations that come.

(3) Similarly, in Matthew 9:28, Jesus conditioned the healing of two blind men upon their answer to this question, "Do you believe *that I am able* to do this?" (emphasis mine).

The fact that God is *able* to do something doesn't unconditionally guarantee that He *will* do it. It may be something He never intends to do. Or He may do it only for those who respond as He commands, as is the case in Jude 24.

To Keep You from Stumbling

This is the only New Testament occurrence of the word translated here as "stumble," and it refers to *losing one's footing, stumbling,* or *falling.* Clearly its use is figurative. Some suggest that only doctrinal slippage is meant, but Jude was warning his readers about false teachers who were promoting *both* false doctrine *and* licentious living (see verses 15-18).

Jude was encouraging believers to look to the One who can keep them from being duped by false teachers (note verses 20-23). To suggest that in verse 24 Jude was unconditionally guaranteeing his readers that they wouldn't be duped is to destroy the whole point of the letter! It was Jude's fear that the false teachers *would* dupe his readers that prompted him to write this letter (see verses 3-4).

To Present You Faultless with Joy

Many commentators take the position that God *guarantees* freedom from stumbling because they conclude from the use of the word *faultless* that eternal salvation must be in view.

One author writes,

> But pursue it [sanctification] we will if we are truly born again, for God Himself guarantees our perseverance in righteousness...He is able to keep you from stumbling, and to make you stand in the presence of His glory blameless with great joy (Jude 24).[4]

---

[4] John F. MacArthur, Jr., *Faith Works: The Gospel According to the Apostles* (Dallas, TX: Word Publishers, 1993), 130. See also his comments about Jude 24 on 180, 185.

Another author relates verse 24 back to verse 21 and says,

> It is noteworthy that when Jude exhorts us to keep ourselves
> in the love of God (v. 21), he concludes with a doxology for
> Him who is able to keep us from falling and who will pres-
> ent us without blemish before the presence of His glory (v.
> 24). The warning passages are *means* which God uses in
> our life to accomplish His purpose in grace.[5]

However, eternal life is eternal. The Lord Jesus promised that
once anyone ate of the bread of life he would *never hunger again*
(John 6:35). Once anyone drank the water of life, he would *never
thirst again* (John 6:35). Never means never. The believer who falls
remains eternally secure. Why? Because God guarantees it! The
moment we come to faith, our eternal salvation is *FDIC* insured:
Father's Declaration Is Certain.

Jude is talking instead about the future judgment of believers at
the Judgment Seat of Christ where the Lord Jesus will present every
believer before the Father. But not all believers will be presented as
"faultless," nor will all believers have "exceeding joy" at the Bema.
Only those believers who have persevered will have such an experience. Compare Matthew 16:27; Mark 8:38; 1 Corinthians 9:27; 2
Corinthians 5:10; and 1 John 2:28.

The word "faultless" (*amomos*) means "without spot" or "without blemish." Sometimes it is used to mean complete sinlessness,
as when it is used in reference to the Lord Jesus (see Hebrews 9:14;
1 Peter 1:19). However, it can also refer to an experience which,
though not sinless, is nevertheless pleasing to God, because it
reflects faithfulness to Him. For example, Revelation 14:5 speaks of
144,000 Jewish evangelists during the Tribulation, "In their mouth
was found no guile, for they are *without fault* [*amomos*] before the
throne of God." Compare also Colossians 1:22 and 2 Peter 3:14.

The same idea, though using a different Greek word (*anenkletos*),
is found in the requirements for elders in the church. Elders and
deacons are men who must be "blameless" in their experience (1

---

[5] Charles Horne, *Salvation* (Chicago, IL: Moody Press, 1971), 95. Note that staying
in God's love is equated with getting into the kingdom. Why couldn't Jude be saying
instead that believers continue to experience God's love only as long as they persevere?
Believers experience God's wrath when they fall away (Romans 13:4-5; Ephesians 5:6-7;
Hebrews 3:11; 4:3).

Timothy 3:10; Titus 1:6-7). Likewise, Elizabeth and Zacharias were said to be "blameless" (*amemptoi*) in their experience (Luke 1:6).

God rewards faithfulness. A special measure of joy at the Judgment Seat of Christ and forever thereafter is waiting for believers who do not lose their footing.

We Can't Blame God

Comedian Flip Wilson used to quip, "The devil made me do it." But for Christians at the Judgment Seat of Christ, no excuses will be valid. We won't be able to legitimately blame the devil, our parents, our spouses, our children, our genes, illness, society, circumstances, or God Himself.[6] Nothing can "make us" stumble from the path of righteousness. If any of us walks away from God, we do so because we have failed to look to Him who is able to keep us from stumbling (cf. Romans 16:25; 2 Peter 3:14-18).

Victory is possible in the Christian life because God is ready, willing, and *able* to sustain us through the temptations and trials we face. The question is not whether He is able to keep us from stumbling. Rather, the question is, whether we will continue to look in faith and obedience to Him who *is* able to keep us from stumbling.

---

[6] This is not to suggest that the Lord Jesus will fail to take these things into account at His Judgment Seat. We will each be evaluated according to our own ability (Matthew 25:15; Luke 12:48; 1 Corinthians 4:1-5). None of us begins the Christian life at precisely the same place morally. Nor do we have the same spiritual gifts, talents, treasure, and opportunity. The Lord will take all of this into account. The point here is that none of these things are excuses for falling away from the Lord. The Lord will keep every Christian who is walking in fellowship with Him from falling away.

CHAPTER 17

Keep Your Eyes on the Prize
(1 Corinthians 9:24-27)

I really cannot give you the formula for success. But I can give you the formula for failure: *Try to please everyone.* That saying by an unknown sage is so true. If you try to please everyone, you are destined to fail.

Studies show that about one in five people you meet don't like you even before you've said anything. They may decide this based simply on your size, shape, color, race, religion, or clothing. Many of them cannot be won over, no matter what you say.

In his famous song "Garden Party," Rick Nelson sang in the climactic last line, "You see, you can't please everyone, so you got to please yourself." Many people feel that way today. Realizing they can't have everyone's approval, they turn to hedonism, whatever makes them feel good.

Most of us admit to having a strong desire for the approval of at least those closest to us. While we can't please all people, we surely want to please the most important people in our lives. At work we want to know that our employers approve of us. That affects how we feel about our job, and whether we receive raises and promotions. Everyone wants the approval of a spouse, for, lacking that, each day becomes a trial.

Parental approval is paramount, because apart from a spouse, no other human's approval means as much as Mom's and Dad's. Studies show that many adults are still trying to please their parents.

In fact, even after Mom and Dad have died, many adults continue to long for that approval.

However, God's approval is the most important approval anyone can have. After all, He is our Creator, the One to whom we are accountable (Hebrews 4:13). As Christians, we will be judged by the Lord Jesus. His approval is something every Christian should strive to gain and maintain.

Assurance of salvation—knowing for sure that you have eternal life and can never lose it—is a vital part of the Christian life. Such assurance produces gratitude and motivates obedience.

Yet many passages, including 1 Corinthians 9:24-27, suggest that if we fail to persevere as believers, we will miss out on something. In this case, that which is potentially forfeited is God's approval. What we are in danger of missing is not the kingdom, but rewards once we get there. While eternal life can't be lost, eternal rewards can be.

Paul Was Sure of His Eternal Destiny

For the many Bible interpreters who do not believe it is possible to be sure that you will enter the kingdom, the idea of seeking God's approval is a salvation issue. Some commentators understand Paul to be expressing doubts in the following passage, about whether or not he would make it to heaven!

> Do you not know that those who run in a race all run, but one receives the prize? Run in such a way that you may obtain it. And everyone who competes for the prize is temperate in all things. Now they do it to obtain a perishable crown, but we for an imperishable crown. Therefore I run thus: not with uncertainty. Thus I fight: not as one who beats the air. But I discipline my body and bring it into subjection, lest, when I have preached to others, I myself should become disqualified (1 Corinthians 9:24-27).

Many believe that Paul was here expressing fear that he might lose eternal life.[1]

---

[1] Concerning 1 Corinthians 9:24-27, Gordon Fee writes: "[Paul] 'disciplined' himself 'for the sake of the gospel,' *so that he, along with them, might share in the promises of the gospel*...But does Paul actually mean that one can fail to obtain the prize? Some would say no, but usually because of a prior theological commitment, not because of what

Others say he feared he might prove he never really *had* eternal life.[2]

Such suggestions concern me. For if the Apostle Paul wasn't sure he was eternally secure, then who *can* be sure? Whether Calvinist or Arminian, such thinking is what I call "daisy theology."

Daisy theology is the view that we can't be sure of our eternal destiny until we die. Remember the young girl plucking off the petals of a daisy? As she pulled off each petal she'd say alternately, "He loves me. He loves me not." She hoped that the one left at the end would be the "He loves me" petal. Sadly, many Christians live like that. They hope that when the sands of their hourglass run out, God will love them and give them entrance into the kingdom.

But didn't Paul elsewhere indicate that he was absolutely certain he was eternally secure (e.g., Romans 8:38-39; Ephesians 2:8-9; 1 Timothy 1:16; 2 Timothy 1:12)? Commentators who think Paul expressed doubts in 1 Corinthians 9:24-27 call this "a tension."[3] I'll say. This type of thinking gives me a tension headache!

---

the text itself says…*It would be sheer folly to suggest that the warnings are not real. Paul keeps warning and assurance in tension.* Simultaneously he *exhorts* and, by this and the following examples, warns the Corinthians of their imminent danger if they do not exercise 'self control' in the matter of idolatry…" (*The First Epistle to the Corinthians,* New International Commentary Series [Grand Rapids, MI: Wm. B. Eerdmans Publishing Company, 1987], 439-40, italics mine).

[2] Charles Hodge wrote concerning verse 27: "He made these strenuous exertions, lest, having preached the gospel to others, he himself should become (*adokimos*) a reprobate, one rejected. What an argument and what a reproof is this! The reckless and listless Corinthians thought they could safely indulge themselves to the very verge of sin, *while this devoted apostle considered himself as engaged in a life-struggle for his salvation*" (*Commentary on the First Epistle to the Corinthians* [Grand Rapids, MI: Wm. B. Eerdmans Publishing Company, Reprinted 1980], 169, italics mine).

Yet Hodge goes on to point to Romans 8:38-39 and to say that Paul not only expressed fears, but also "the most joyful assurance of salvation" (169). How are doubts and assurance harmonized in one mind? He suggests that, "the one state of mind is the necessary condition of the other. It is only those who are conscious of this constant and deadly struggle with sin, to whom this assurance is given" (169).

See also *The New Geneva Study Bible: Bringing the Light of the Reformation to Scripture* (Nashville, TN: Thomas Nelson Publishers, 1995), 1811. A note indicates: "It would be wrong to dismiss or minimize Paul's concern (cf. 15:2; Phil. 3:11; Col. 1:23) by suggesting that it is merely hypothetical or relates only to rewards and not salvation. Paul was confident that absolutely nothing would be able to separate him from God's love (Rom. 8:38-39), *but he never presumed that he was saved regardless of what he did.* No Christian can afford to take lightly the warnings of Scripture (10:12)" (emphasis mine).

[3] In essence they are saying that assurance is trumped by warnings.

Most in Christendom believe that no one can be sure before he dies that he will get into the kingdom. The reason is that any one of us could fail to persevere.

I don't know if I can say strongly enough how much this view of "assurance" grieves me. Of course, the idea that we must persevere to get into the kingdom not only destroys assurance, but it destroys the good news as well. In most churches today, pastors across denominational lines, are teaching that perseverance is a condition of entering the kingdom. Unfortunately this is also true of the vast majority of seminary and Bible college professors. That is doubly sad because they are training the *next* generation of pastors and teachers. This trend will only increase unless the Lord raises up concerned individuals to proclaim the truth with love and conviction.

Leon Morris holds to the Reformed Doctrine of the Perseverance of the Saints—the belief that all genuine Christians will persevere in faith and good works. Thus it is especially significant that he does not see assurance in view in this passage. Commenting on 1 Corinthians 9:27, Morris said:

> Paul's fear was not that he might lose his salvation, but that he might suffer loss *through failing to satisfy his Lord* (cf. 3:15).[4]

He had this to say about 1 Corinthians 3:15:

> *He will suffer loss* means he will lose his wage, a workman fined for poor workmanship. Being saved "as through fire" (RSV) may have been a proverbial expression to indicate one is saved and no more.[5]

Paul had eternal life and knew it. He didn't fear he might not make it into the kingdom. And neither should any of us who believe in Christ. It is impossible for one who believes in Christ to fail to make it into the kingdom, for God guarantees it, whether we persevere or not (John 6:35-40; 11:25-27).

Eternal salvation is a gift—not a prize to be won for work done.

---

[4] Leon Morris, *1 Corinthians*, revised edition, Tyndale New Testament Commentaries (Grand Rapids, MI: Wm. B. Eerdmans Publishing Company, 1958, 1985), 138, italics mine.

[5] Ibid., 66, italics his.

Perseverance Required for the Prize

The imagery Paul presents in 1 Corinthians 9:24-27 is that of athletic competition. Possibly Paul was thinking specifically of the Isthmian Games, athletic contests held every two years near Corinth. They were similar to the Olympics of today, and included running and boxing events.

In athletic events such as these, all participants are part of the competition, but only one wins. In that day the prize was a pine wreath.[6]

In the Christian race, believers work *with* each other, not against each other. *All* Christians can win in the Christian life. In fact, the more we help each other, the more we will all win. The prize for which we Christians strive is imperishable. It will never fade away or be destroyed by time or death. It is eternal.

I ran track during high school and college. In 1995 when I turned forty-three, I decided to take up the sport again. After joining the Master's division of the U.S. Track and Field Association, I competed in races in and around the Dallas area. What a joy it was to run fast again and even to win a medal on occasion! However, as impressive as the medals are to look at, they are only a temporary pleasure.

Paul knew that Christ approved of him (see 1 Corinthians 3:5-9; 4:1, 11-13, 16; 9:1-23; 11:1)[7] because he knew he was faithfully serving

---

[6] Professor Oscar Broneer, Director of the American School of Archaeology, says: "The prize of victory at Isthmia was a wreath, at first made of pine, but in the fifth century B.C. a wreath of wild celery was introduced. In late Hellenistic times and in the Roman era, both types of wreaths were awarded to victors in the Games. The celery of the Isthmian crown was withered, in contrast to the Nemean which was made of fresh celery. The withered wreath bestowed upon winners at Isthmia may have lent color to the Apostle Paul's statement in his first Epistle to the Corinthians (9.25), where he contrasts the 'imperishable wreath' ('incorruptible crown' in the King James version), which the Christians receive, with the 'perishable wreath' of the athletes. Paul may well have been at Isthmus for the celebration of the Games in the year 51, when he lived and worked as tent-maker in Corinth." http://www.ioa.org.gr/uploads/Young%20 Participants%201970~37989-600-2(1).pdf, p. 98.

[7] It is true that nowhere does Paul specifically use the term *approved* in any of these verses. However, the concept is clearly present in those texts. It is instructive to compare Romans 16:10 where Paul says of a member of the Church of Rome: "Greet Apelles, *approved* in Christ" (emphasis mine). He does not say *Greet Apelles who will be approved if he perseveres*. No, he speaks of him as being an approved Christian worker at the time of the writing of the epistle. Surely if he called one who worked under him "approved in Christ" he knew himself to be approved as well. However, as the case of

Him. But would he maintain Christ's approval to the end of his life? Paul could not be sure, for he knew he had to persevere to retain that approval. And he knew that no Christian, not even he himself, could be sure he would persevere.

The Prize for Perseverance

The Lord Jesus will give an imperishable crown to those believers whom He approves. Elsewhere Paul said, "If we endure, we shall also reign with Him" (2 Timothy 2:12a). Ruling with Christ is a privilege every believer should desire. It should motivate us to persevere in a life of faith. Paul had his eyes on the prize. Do you?

Conclusion

Alfred Rascon was an Army Medic in Vietnam on March 16, 1966, when his unit came under fire so intense that Rascon later called it "ten minutes of pure hell." While helping a fatally wounded machine gunner, Rascon took a bullet in the back that nearly penetrated his spine. He had good reason to quit and wait for medical evacuation. But he could still move, so he pressed on. Under heavy fire, Rascon took ammunition to another machine gunner. While delivering the ammo, a grenade went off at his feet and he was hit in the head, wounding him in the mouth, nose, and ears. He certainly had every reason to quit now.

When another grenade landed, Rascon fell on a fellow soldier, absorbing the blow. Surely now he would quit. He got up and saw another grenade land near his wounded staff sergeant. Again Rascon fell on his comrade and took the shrapnel himself.

At this point he could barely walk. Yet he had no give-up in him. On he went.

"And then," said President Bill Clinton in his February 8, 2000 Congressional Medal of Honor award ceremony at the White House, "barely able to walk, bleeding from his ears and nose, he ran to recover a machine gun that the enemy was about to capture. The extra firepower kept the enemy from advancing, and Alfred Rascon saved his platoon."

Demas shows (compare Colossians 4:14; Philemon 24; and 2 Timothy 4:10), one who is an approved workman may forfeit that status. See my article "Demas Has Forsaken Me," available at www.faithalone.org/magazine/y1995/95A2.html.

Time and time again Alfred could have given up. But with the strength he had left, he kept risking his life to save others. He was responsible for saving many men in his platoon, if not the entire platoon, as the President's remarks suggested.

Amazingly, Rascon recovered from his wounds and not only completed that tour in Vietnam, but served a second tour as well. He remained in the Army until 1976. Since that time he has continued in government service.

Am I that committed in my service for the Lord Jesus Christ? Is there give-up in me? Or am I in this for the long haul? We need to ask ourselves these questions. The Lord Jesus may well return any day now. But if He should tarry for several decades, will we persevere?

God places a premium on ending well. It is important that we persevere in our service for Christ. Quitters will not receive His approval. While eternal life is received the moment we believe in Christ and is secure forever, approval is received only by putting our faith to work. Approval can be lost. Our aim should be to maintain a standing of full approval, maximizing our lives for Christ so that we will hear those blessed words, "Well done, good and faithful servant."

Section 5
Appendixes

If, after reading
The Road to Reward,
you still have questions,
the following appendixes have been written
with you in mind.
Bob Wilkin

Won't All Believers Be Equally Rewarded? (Matthew 20:1-16)

A leading New Testament scholar writes concerning the Parable of the Day Laborers (Matthew 20:1-16): "Almost everyone agrees that Jesus is teaching about a fundamental equality here among those who are truly his disciples. All are rewarded alike."[1]

Let's take a minute to review the particulars of this parable.

Early one morning a landowner hired a group of laborers to work in his vineyard all day for one denarius each. At 9:00 a.m. he chose another group to go work and told them he would pay them whatever was right. Again he went out at about noon and 3:00 p.m., and hired two more groups. At about 5:00 p.m. he went out and found another group that no one had hired. He sent them to the vineyard, and promised to pay them whatever was right. At the end of the day, when it was time to pay the workers, he paid those who only worked one hour one denarius each. When the first group came, they expected to receive more, even though they had agreed to work for one denarius. "They complained against the landowner, saying 'These last men have worked only one hour, and you made them equal to us who have borne the burden and the heat of the day.'" The landowner's response was, "Friend, I am doing you no wrong. Did you not agree with me for a denarius? Take what is yours and go your way. I wish to give this last man the same as to

---

[1] Craig L. Blomberg, "Degrees of Reward in the Kingdom of Heaven?" *Journal of the Evangelical Theological Society* (June 1992): 160.

you. Is it not lawful for me to do what I wish with my own things? Or is your eye evil because I am good?"

This parable does seem to teach that everyone will be equally rewarded. However, we know from many other texts that this is not the case. The real lesson of the parable is that those believers *who have served Him faithfully for their entire Christian lives,* will be rewarded equally *regardless of the length of their Christian lives.*

All five groups represent believers who heed the call of discipleship from the start of their Christian experience. That is evident by the fact that as soon as they were hired, they all went to work. What distinguishes their length of service is how long they were Christians before death or the Rapture.

The length of time one is born again prior to death or the Rapture is not a limiting factor in how he will be rewarded.[2] The person who served Christ faithfully for the *one year* he was a Christian will be equally rewarded with someone who served Christ for *eighty years.* Of course, this assumes both people served the Lord wholeheartedly during that time. (Admittedly that is a variable the Lord does not discuss in this parable.) The Lord can and will extrapolate what we would have done if we had had more time.

When I was on staff with Campus Crusade for Christ, we were seeking to fulfill the Great Commission in the U.S. by the end of 1976, and in the world by the end of 1980. In 1977, when I was considering leaving staff to attend seminary, I remember expressing my concern to Josh McDowell that I didn't want to miss out on ministry while I prepared to minister. But I really believed I would be able to serve the Lord more effectively if I had a theological education. I felt torn.

His response to me was that there would always be people to win for Christ and that I should go to seminary.

Later, while in seminary, a student asked one of our professors what would happen if the Rapture occurred while we were in school. Wouldn't we miss out on rewards over those who chose to keep on ministering without seminary?

---

[2] Note that I didn't say that the length of time one *serves* is not a limiting factor in how much we are rewarded. For length of service may well be a limiting factor in rewards. The person who was a Christian for thirty years but only served for the last ten would not be as highly rewarded as one who served Christ faithfully his entire Christian life (however long that was). Only in cases where length of service coincides with length of time one is a believer is length of service not a limiting factor.

"No, you wouldn't," said the professor. "There surely will be many in seminary at the time of the Rapture. That doesn't mean that preparation is unwise. We all are to do our best in serving Christ. For some that includes special training for ministry. Should the Lord come when you are in school, He will take into account not only what you have done, but what you have prepared to do. He knows what you would have done had you had a full life."

The Parable of the Day Laborers in Matthew 20 is not an invitation to start serving Christ whenever we feel like it. Rather, it is an encouragement that no matter how long it is between our new birth and the time we go to be with the Lord, He will reward us fairly. We need not dread the Rapture as though it could snatch away our opportunity to rule with Christ and to have treasure in heaven. Be faithful and follow Christ. He will reward us fairly.

Won't This Lead to Jealousy in the Kingdom?

C hildren have a very hard time with jealousy. "He got more ice cream than I did!" "I want a bike like Suzy got for her birthday!" The more we mature, of course, the less jealousy we should experience; but to one degree or another, jealousy is a problem for all of us.

One question that I have heard repeatedly as I have taught on rewards is, "If some will have more than others in the kingdom, won't this lead to jealousy?"

Will We Be Jealous of Jesus?

It should be obvious that the Lord Jesus will have more reward than anyone else in the kingdom. After all, He is the King of kings and Lord of lords who will rule over the entire world. The wealth of the universe will be His. Does that mean some might be jealous of Him? Hardly! Remember, if degrees of honor, glory, possessions, and power necessarily result in jealousy, then we would all be forever jealous of the Lord Jesus!

Based on the writings of Ezekiel, many believe that David will be prince forever over the nation of Israel. That means he will be Jesus' right-hand man in the rulership over Israel.

We also know from the Gospels that the Apostles will sit on twelve thrones and rule over the twelve tribes of Israel. Evidently they will serve under the direction of David. Thus David will have more authority than they will and they will have more authority than the citizens of Israel over whom they rule.

Yet no one will be jealous of David or the Apostles or a host of others who have earned the right to these exalted positions.

No Jealousy, No Sin

We need to realize that in the kingdom we will be free from what Paul calls *the flesh*. While they will be real, our glorified bodies will be immortal and incapable of sinning.

Even though Augustine was not always clear on the gospel, what he had to say 1,500 years ago on the subject of degrees of reward and potential envy is worth heeding:

> But who can conceive, not to say describe, what degrees of honour and glory shall be awarded to the various degrees of merit? Yet it cannot be doubted that there shall be degrees. And in that blessed city there shall be this great blessing, that no inferior shall envy any superior, as now the archangels are not envied by the angels, because no one will wish to be what he has not received, though bound in the strictest concord with him who has received; as in the body the finger does not seek to be the eye, though both members are harmoniously included in the complete structure of the body. And thus, along with his gift, greater or less, each shall receive this further gift of contentment to desire no more than he has.[1]

Everyone in the eternal kingdom will certainly be content. However, there is a sense in which we might feel regret if we fail to rule with Christ, or if we rule to a much lesser degree than we might have because we squandered our chance to do more for Him during our lifetime.

So, we dare not slough off the idea of rewards on the grounds that it will result in jealousy. As we say here in Texas, "That dog won't hunt." Rather than looking for an excuse not to do our best for Christ, let's get busy and work hard for Him (2 Timothy 2:6). We'll be forever glad if we do.

---

[1] Augustine, *The City of God*, Bk. 22.30.

Whatever Happened to the New Earth? (Revelation 21-22)

Even though God has told us about eternity, I've found that most Christians have very little idea of what eternity will be like. Most Christians seem to think that this life is much more exciting and enjoyable than eternity will be. *Many believers think of leaving this life as a dreadful thing.*

If we gain a clear picture of what eternity will be like, it has a profound effect on how we live now. It energizes and motivates us. My own studies of this topic have had a profound effect upon me.

Most Christians look forward to heaven, not the new earth. If you asked them where they will spend eternity, they would say, "Well in heaven, of course."

During my seminary days my wife and I were walking one night with another seminary couple. I mentioned how much I looked forward to spending eternity in heaven. My friend, Will Nece, surprised me when he said, "Why on earth are you looking forward to heaven? We won't spend eternity in heaven. Believers will spend eternity on the new earth."

Things came together for me at that time and they have profoundly improved my concept of eternity future.

If Adam and Eve Had Not Sinned Mankind Would Have Lived Forever on the Pre-Fall, Pre-Flood Earth

I believe that if we want to understand what God wanted for mankind, we need to go back to the beginning. What would have happened if Adam and Eve had not sinned?

Gen 1:26-28 says:

> Then God said, "Let Us make man in Our image, according to Our likeness; let them have dominion over the fish of the sea, over the birds of the air, and over the cattle, over all the earth and over every creeping thing that creeps on the earth." So God created man in His *own* image; in the image of God He created him; male and female He created them. Then God blessed them, and God said to them, "Be fruitful and multiply; fill the earth and subdue it; have dominion over the fish of the sea, over the birds of the air, and over every living thing that moves on the earth."

If Adam and Eve had not sinned, then they would have been fruitful and multiplied and filled the earth with tens or hundreds of billions of people. There would have been no death.

Eternity would have taken place on earth! Not the precise earth we live on today. This planet has been cursed. But they would have lived forever on a glorious earth.

> Then to Adam He said, "Because you have heeded the voice of your wife, and have eaten from the tree of which I commanded you, saying, 'You shall not eat of it':
> "Cursed is the ground for your sake;
> In toil you shall eat of it
> All the days of your life.
> Both thorns and thistles it shall bring forth for you,
> And you shall eat the herb of the field.
> In the sweat of your face you shall eat bread
> Till you return to the ground,
> For out of it you were taken;
> For dust you are,
> And to dust you shall return" (Gen 3:17-19).

Time doesn't permit looking at Genesis 6 and following and developing the terrible effects of Noah's flood. The point is, the fallen earth before the flood was much better than the earth we live on now. Before the flood men routinely lived 900+ years. After the flood, lifespans were quickly cut ten fold.

My point is this. Our earth today is only a shadow of what it once was. It is only a caricature of what God intended. *But this planet is where mankind would have spent eternity if Adam and Eve had not sinned.*

Of course, it would be better than this earth is. The planet changed drastically after Noah's flood. But it would be *this* earth, just with better worldwide climate, terrain, no weeds, no pests, no wild animals, etc.

Shouldn't that make us question the assumption that our eternal destiny is spent in heaven? If humans were not created with heaven in mind, why do we think that is where we will spend eternity?

I believe the reason Christians adopted this view is because of Plato and Aristotle who taught that matter and the material world is bad and the spirit and the spirit world is good. Thus their idea of a blessed afterlife was one in which people were freed from bodies, earth, and anything of substance. But that is not at all what the Bible teaches. Abraham was not anticipating a disembodied ethereal experience. He anticipated being raised from the dead and living in the Promised Land under the rulership of the Messiah. So did David and so did all of the OT saints. So should we.

God's Plan for Man Living on Earth with Jesus Will Not Be Thwarted

Now I saw a new heaven and a new earth, for the first heaven and the first earth had passed away. Also there was no more sea. Then I, John, saw the holy city, New Jerusalem, coming down out of heaven from God, prepared as a bride adorned for her husband. And I heard a loud voice from heaven saying,

> Behold, the tabernacle of God *is* with men, and He will dwell with them, and they shall be His people. God Himself will be with them *and be* their God. And God will wipe away every tear from their eyes; there shall be no more death, nor sorrow, nor crying. There shall be no more pain, for the former things have passed away (Rev 21:1-4).

In Rev 21:1-4 we read about how God will reverse the curses of Gen 3:17-19. The new earth will be free from death, sin, disease, a ground that fights us, wild animals, pests, etc.

Jesus will not rule *from heaven* forever. He will forever rule *from the New Jerusalem on the New Earth*.

Revelation 21-22 shows that what Gen 3:8 anticipated will soon be realized on the new earth. The Lord Jesus will live with us forever, but not on a fallen earth, but a new and unfallen earth.

Believers will have real bodies. We will serve a living Savior with our bodies, not merely with our minds. We will serve Him on the new earth.

Heaven at Most Will Be a Place We Visit

My friend Will was right. The New Jerusalem comes down from the new heavens and lands on the new earth.

Revelation 21:24 shows that the kings of the nations on the new earth will bring their tribute to Jesus in the New Jerusalem.

There will be nations on this planet. There will be a glorious kingdom.

We will not live in heaven.

It is possible we will visit there. The Bible doesn't say. However, we will live with our Savior and Lord and King on the new earth.

Likely the Only Extended Time Any Believer Will Spend in Heaven Is If He Dies Before the Rapture.

It is true that if a believer dies before the Rapture, he goes to heaven to be with Christ and our fellow believers. Philippians 1:23 makes that clear ("Having a desire to depart and be with Christ, which is far better").

According to 1 Thess 4:17 the dead in Christ will rise first. They will come down from heaven as we who are alive go up from earth. We meet in the middle, "in the air."

We will spend the seven years of the Tribulation with the Lord, either in the clouds or in heaven. Either way, after the Tribulation we will be with the Lord for 1000 years on the Millennial Earth. After that, we will spend eternity with the Lord on the new earth.

In my new book, *The Ten Most Misunderstood Words in the Bible,* I have a chapter on heaven in which I discuss the points I am making today. The song entitled, "This World Is Not My Home" has things backwards:

> This world is not my home;
> I'm just a passing through.
> My treasures are laid up
> Somewhere beyond the blue.
> The angels beckon me
> From heaven's open door.
> And I can't feel at home
> In the world anymore.

Now if by this world the hymn writer had meant *the cursed post-fall earth*, he is right. But if he means *earth*, then he is greatly mistaken. And it is clear that he does mean that when he goes on to say, "If heaven's not my home, then Lord what will I do." Even if we ignore the lack of assurance evident in that line, we are still left with a song that mistakenly sees heaven and not the new earth as our eternal home.

In reality we go from this earth to the cleaned up and improved Millennial earth and then to the new earth. Actually the song would better read just the opposite:

> Heaven is not my home;
> I'm just a passing through.
> My treasures are laid up
> Somewhere beyond the blue.
> One day soon I'll meet Him
> In the air above.
> Then He take me with Him,
> To Earth's open door.

Immortality in Perfect Glorified Bodies

Look at John 11:25-27.

> Jesus said to her, "I am the resurrection and the life. He who believes in Me, though he may die, he shall live. And whoever lives and believes in Me shall never die. Do you believe

this?" She said to Him, "Yes, Lord, I believe that You are the Christ, the Son of God, who is to come into the world."

What does "he shall live" mean in 11:25? Answer: It means he will live physically. This is the promise of bodily resurrection. This was Job's belief in Job 19:25 and Daniel's in Daniel 12.

This earth will be destroyed so that a new and untainted earth, the new earth, can take its place (2 Pet 3:10-13; Rev 21:1-3).

We were made to walk and to run and use our limbs and to think and speak and serve. We weren't made to float on clouds somewhere. We weren't made for heaven! We were made for earth!

The fact that our first parents sinned meant God would have to create a new heavens and a new earth. And He will.

Jesus will reign on earth as the Godhead always intended. There will be no traces of sin or the curse on this new planet and indeed not in the entire new heavens, the new stars and planets.

I imagine we will do lots of space travel. We may colonize planets. We aren't told.

But whatever Jesus has us doing, it will be what we were created to do. We will use these bodies and our new earth to glorify our Savior and Lord and King forever.

I don't know about you. But it excites me to realize that I'm not done with a physical existence when this life is over. What I get is the perfect physical existence God always wanted for us and we always wanted.

The doctrine of eternal rewards is more exciting if we realize that our eternal experience will occur in a glorified body on a glorified earth in a glorified universe.

What Will We Do in Eternity?

We will serve Christ forever (Rev 22:3). Some will rule with Him. That evidently will be their primary task. Others will not rule, but they too will serve.

Work is not a bad word. We were made to be productive and creative.

Some jobs that likely will still be done: painters, sculptors, writers, engineers, architects, singers, musicians, farmers, contractors, chefs, small business owners, etc.

Some jobs will no longer be available: policemen, prison guards, pest control, wild animal tamers, doctors, lawyers, psychologists, etc.

I imagine that there will be amazing art work in eternity future and we will all have better appreciation for art. The music will be fantastic, and again with greater appreciation. The books and plays will be great. The roads and buildings will be far better. Transportation will be amazing.

Our lives will be fulfilling then. Of course, the more we've done for Christ now, the more abundant our lives will be on the new earth. But everyone will be content and joyful.

Applications

- Rejoice daily in your guaranteed eternal destiny (John 5:24).
- Let your groanings over your fallen body (2 Cor 5:2, 4) cause you to long daily for a glorified body and for the soon return of Christ.
- Live each day in light of the Judgment Seat of Christ, which will occur after the Lord returns for us (2 Cor 5:9-11).
- Teach your children and friends and loved ones about the promise of bodily resurrection and the promise of the New Earth. This is a much neglected aspect of evangelism and of discipleship.

Conclusion

So what's my point: *Live every day in light of eternity.* The idea that someone can be so heavenly minded as to be no earthly good is ridiculous. If we have a good grasp of what eternity will be like, we will be highly motivated to be extremely practical in this life.

While we live *in* this world, we are not *of this world.* If we see our aim as this life and not the life to come, then we will not live this life as God intended.

There's nothing wrong with trying to help others. But we do that best by realizing the Jesus is coming again soon and then He will establish righteousness and peace on earth. We live this life best if we recall it is a vapor and that the life to come is not.

Everything we do will be influenced if we keep the big picture in mind.

Live each day in light of eternity. Christ is coming again. It could be today. It surely is soon. Live in such a way each day that you are storing up an abundant eternal experience. What a joy it would be to hear Him say, "Well done, good and faithful servant." Let's pray.

Take Heed How You Hear
(Luke 8:11-18)

There are many Biblical verses that are wrongly used to teach that salvation and assurance of salvation depend upon our works. Many preachers fail to rightly divide the Word and properly distinguish between evangelistic passages from discipleship passages. Luke 8:11-18 is the Lord's interpretation of the Parable of the Four Soils,

"Now the parable is this: The seed is the word of God. Those by the wayside are the ones who hear; then the devil comes and takes away the word out of their hearts, lest they should believe and be saved. But the ones on the rock are those who, when they hear, receive the word with joy; and these have no root, who believe for a while and in time of temptation fall away. Now the ones that fell among thorns are those who, when they have heard, go out and are choked with cares, riches, and pleasures of life, and bring no fruit to maturity. But the ones that fell on the good ground are those who, having heard the word with a noble and good heart keep it and bear fruit with patience. No one, when has lit a lamp, covers it with a vessel or puts it under a bed, but sets it on a lampstand, that those who enter may see the light. For nothing is secret that will not be revealed nor anything hidden that will not be known and come to light. Therefore take heed how you hear. For whoever has, to him more will be given; and whoever does not have, even what he seems to have will be taken from him."

People, believers and unbelievers, don't always listen well to what God says in His Word. In fact, as we will see in this parable, some stop listening entirely, some listen but distractedly, and only some listen well to what God is saying.

In order to understand this parable, there are two key interpretive questions to ask about each soil.

First, is the Lord referring to a regenerate or an unregenerate person? The answer to that question will determine how we interpret and apply the parable. Most people don't give this much thought. The answer seems quite obvious to them.

Second, why are there two extra soils? Why not just one soil representing an unbeliever and another representing a believer? There must be a reason why the Lord gave four soils instead of two. We will consider that as we examine the details.

The Most Common Understanding

The most common approach to the parable is that only one soil (soil four) represents born-again people. The other three soils are different kinds of unbelievers. This can be broken down into two different views.

The Loss of Salvation View

If it is true that born again people can lose eternal life, then obviously soil two is a person who loses his salvation since he falls away. Likewise, soil three would also be a person who loses his salvation. Even though he doesn't fall away, he doesn't bring fruit to maturity.

In the Arminian loss of salvation view, soils two, three, and four are all believers, but only the fourth soil is a good believer who keeps his salvation.

The False Professor View

In this view, a born-again person can't lose eternal life, but only believers who persevere to death in faith and good works are truly regenerate.

Thus, according to this view, the second soil is clearly one who is a false professor. He has what they call *temporary faith*. He believes in Jesus as his Savior for a time, but then in time of temptation he falls away. His failure to persevere proves he was never really born again.

According to this view the third soil probably represents a different type of false professor. This is someone who seems to serve Christ all the way to the grave, but the person is half-hearted in his service. He is distracted by cares, riches, and pleasures. This half-heartedness shows that he was probably never born again in the first place.

The fourth soil is viewed as someone who is truly born again since he perseveres in faith and good works to the end.

While the "false professor" view is quite similar to the "loss of salvation" view, it differs in that soils two and three are viewed not as believers who lost their salvation, but as false professors who were never saved in the first place.

However, both of these views suggest that only soil four actually makes it to the kingdom.

Another Option: Soils Two, Three, and Four All Represent Believers

According to this view only the first soil represents unbelievers, while the other three represent three different types of regenerate people.

Of course, in order to adopt this view, one must not believe that perseverance in faith and good works is a condition of entering the kingdom.

How Do We Decide Which Is Correct?

Instead of trying to answer this question right now, let's think about *how we find the answer.* What is the proper way to answer interpretive questions?

Prayer is vital. Ask God to show you the truth. Be open to Him showing you.

Observing carefully what is said is also vital. Remember that Jesus said, "Take heed how you hear." That applies to all Scripture, but especially to the parable that immediately precedes that saying.

So we should carefully observe the parable, starting back in the telling of it in Luke 8:5-8, and then also in the interpretation by the Lord in Luke 8:11-15.

We won't do that yet. But let me say that many skip this step when the interpretation seems obvious to them. That is dangerous. If we fail to observe carefully what the Lord said, then we are not "taking heed how we hear." So let's start by making some observations both from the parable and the Lord's explanation of it. In order to answer the question about who each soil represents, let's look at verses 5-8 and 11-15.

Observations from the Text

Springing Up and Not Springing Up (Luke 8:5-8)

Plant life begins at germination, right? But unless we are growing a plant in a box with a glass wall, we can't see germination occur. We don't know that life exists until the green shoot springs forth from the ground. But once it springs forth, we know the seed germinated and life exists.

In verses 6, 7, and 8 the words "it sprang up" jump out at the reader/listener who is taking heed how he hears. The Lord indicates that soil one never sprang up and that soils two, three, and four all sprang up. This suggests that the Lord is comparing three different ways in which regenerate people respond to God's Word throughout their lives.

But what about His explanation of the parable? What does the Lord say to help us?

Believing and Not Believing (Luke 8:12, 13)

The Lord says that soil one does not believe. Indeed, He says more than that. He says that Satan snatches away the seed *lest he should believe and be saved*. According to the Lord, to believe His word is to be saved.

The Lord says that the second soil believes. This must mean that he was saved. Compare verse 13 with verse 12. Now the fact that he later stops believing cannot mean that he was never saved in the first place. It could mean that he has lost eternal life, if that is something that Jesus taught is possible. However, if Jesus taught that eternal life is eternal life, and He did (see John 5:24; 6:35; 11:26), then even the second soil represents a born again person. This person ends up in the kingdom, in spite of the fact that he only believes for a time.

The Progression from Worst to Best (Luke 8:5-8 & Luke 8:12-15)

Clearly soil two is better than soil one. It sprang up, whereas soil one did not. Soil two believed. Soil one did not.

But just as clearly, soil three is better than soil two. While they both sprang up, soil two "withered away because it lacked moisture" (verse 6). Soil three, however, did not wither away. Whereas soil two "fell away" (verse 13), soil three did not fall away. Soil three persevered to the end of life in faith and good works.

Clearly soil four is better than soil three. While they both sprang up, soil three was "choked" by "the thorns," which the Lord later calls "cares, riches, and the pleasures of life" (verse 14). Soil three brings forth fruit, but not mature fruit. The third soil is not called *the good ground* (verse 15). The third soil is not said to have "a noble and good heart."

Therefore, if soil two believed, so did soils three and four, even though the Lord does not specifically mention that. It is obvious that they must have believed because they too "sprang up."

Conclusions from Our Observations

From these observations we may make the following conclusions. The first soil never believed or became born again. The second soil believed, was born again, but then failed in the Christian life. The third soil believed, was born again, but then went on to live a half-hearted Christian life. And finally, the fourth soil believed, was born again, and lived a whole-hearted Christian life.

Unbelievers Don't Believe
and Aren't Saved (Luke 8:5, 12)

The first soil is the one on the path. Its seeds get devoured by birds (verse 5). The Lord interprets that to mean that Satan snatches away the word of life lest they should believe it and be saved (verse 12).

This means the person who never comes to faith in Christ will be eternally condemned. Step one in heeding God's Word is believing in Christ alone for eternal life.

Sadly many today don't believe what God says about what we must do to gain eternal life. Instead of believing in God's free grace in Christ, they think they must commit themselves, turn from their sins, live a good life, go to church, give money, and do other works in order to have eternal life. But since that isn't what God says. Satan has, in effect, snatched away the seed.

Christian growth can't start until the seed germinates.

The Non-Persevering Believer:
Beware of Falling Away (Luke 8:6, 13)

The second soil represents the first type of believer. He is one who heeds the word, but only for a time. The rocky soil sprang up (verse 6). We know that a new plant can spring up from the soil after the seed has germinated. Even if the shoot dies quickly, we know the seed has still germinated. We know there was life.

Likewise, there is no time requirement on saving faith. The moment a person believes the gospel he gains eternal life which can never be lost.

Consider an example. Sally is driving down the road on the way to lunch. She hears an evangelist on a Christian radio station who makes the message of John 3:16 clear. For the first time she understands that eternal life is a free gift and that it is received simply by believing in Jesus Christ for it. She knows she has eternal life because she knows He guarantees it to every believer. Seconds after this joyful experience, a drunk driver crosses the median and hits her head on, killing her instantly. Is there anyone who would say she goes to hell because her faith didn't last but a few seconds?

Now what if we change the story so that she survived the crash, but later stopped believing in Christ. Where would she go then?

To say that all who "truly" believe continue to believe for the rest of their lives is unbiblical. This parable shows it. Once a person believes, he is saved, even if he doesn't put his roots down deep. Saving faith is not necessarily permanent, but eternal life is permanent; the faith that immediately results in eternal life needs to be cultivated in order for it to continue.

So how do we avoid the trap of the person who falls away from the faith? Realize it could happen to you. I know it could happen to me. Don't think you are too spiritual or too wise or too good for that to happen to you. God resists the proud, but gives grace to the humble (James 4:6; 1 Peter 5:5).

A crucial way to avoid falling away is found in verse 18: *keep listening to the Word of God*. Paul put it this way in Gal 2:20, "[we] live by faith in the Son of God." The more we walk in faith, the stronger we become spiritually. This life has the Lord Jesus Christ as its constant focus.

I could also mention some other things which cause your roots to go deep, like:

- Be a regular part of a solid Bible-teaching church (Hebrews 10:23-25).
- Pray without ceasing (1 Thessalonians 5:17).
- Read and meditate on the Word of God (Psalm 1).
- Be honest and open with God (1 John 1:9).
- Avoid false teachers and false teaching (Galatians 1:8-9).
- Focus daily on the return of Christ (Galatians 6:9).

However, none of these things in and of themselves will cause you to grow. If done in the flesh, these things become legalistic observances. They might keep you from falling away, but they won't allow you to maximize your life unless they are done by faith.

The Half-Hearted Believer:
Beware of the Weeds (Luke 8:7, 14)

Not all believers who persevere maximize their lives for Christ. Note the difference between Luke 19:17 and Luke 19:19. One maximizes. One doesn't. Likewise, the third soil "bring[s] no fruit *to maturity*" (italics added). There is fruit, but it is not fully developed. It is choked by the weeds. What are the weeds? Three things: cares, riches, pleasures.

At first thought, only *cares* makes sense. Of course, cares can bring us down if we aren't vigilant. We can become distracted and halfhearted in our service. When cares hit, take them to the Lord. Cast your cares on Him (1 Peter 5:7).

The second type of weed is *riches*. We might think that riches are good. How could riches hurt us? Think again. Riches are very dangerous. We may joke, "I know Lord, that riches are tough to handle. But try me." But we shouldn't joke like that. If God gives us riches, fine. But don't make that your goal.

Handle riches like weeds. Get rid of your riches by giving them away. Once you have enough to live on and enough for retirement and your children's inheritance, why accumulate more savings? Give.

The third type of weed is *the pleasures of life*. Again, we might think pleasures are good. I think the Lord here is thinking of lawful pleasures, not sinful ones. Things like fishing, hunting, golf, television, video games, tennis, skiing, etc. Our pleasures can become a snare if they capture too much of our time and too much of our hearts.

Are your pleasures recreational, or do they weigh you down? If they are hurting your walk with Christ, it is time to weed out that pleasure.

Three common suggestions on dealing with all three:

1. Pray about your cares, riches, pleasures.
2. Live each day in light of eternity. That is, view your cares, riches, and pleasures in that light.
3. Give away your cares, your riches, and your pleasures. You don't want too much of any of those.

The Wholehearted Believer:
Listen Well with a Good Heart (Luke 8:8, 15)

Listen with a noble and good heart. How do we get a good heart? God keeps improving, transforming, the one we have. The key to the Christian life, if there is one, is right here: Be transformed *by the renewal of your mind.* Change of behavior comes from change of thinking (Romans 12:1-2; see also Ephesians 4:23; 2 Corinthians 3:18).

This type of Christian, like the third soil, perseveres. Unlike the third soil, this type of believer is not hindered by cares, riches, pleasures. The result is mature fruit, abundant rewards, and a Luke 19:17 type of servant.

Don't make it your aim to be a half-hearted servant of Christ who perseveres but only accomplishes a fraction of what you could. Be wholehearted.

The Application of the Parable: How We Respond to God Is Vitally Important to Our Well-Being (Luke 8:16-18)

This is one of the few parables where the Lord not only interprets it for us, but He even *applies it for us.* The key words are *take heed how you hear.* In verse 17, a light is used to reveal what otherwise would be hidden.

Verse 17 takes this principle and applies it to the believer and unbeliever. Everything we have said and done, and everything we will do or say, will be revealed. All will be judged according to their works: believers will be judged at the Bema (i.e., the Judgment Seat of Christ), and unbelievers will be judged at the Great White Throne Judgment. Someday all the works of all people will be brought to light.

Verse 18 gives the sobering application: *therefore, take heed how you hear.*

Hearing doesn't just mean that you can pass a quiz on the content. It means that you are applying what God says. Like being one who hears the Word in James 1-2.

The more we hear, the more we will receive. That is true now, so that the one who hears God's Word grows in his understanding and application of it. He becomes more mature. His life becomes more abundant.

The one who doesn't hear goes backwards. His life becomes less abundant. What he has is taken away, and he may even lose his understanding of the Word.

This also will apply at the Bema. The one who has heard well, will be given more at the Bema. The one who has not heard well, will have what he has had taken away. He may find himself demoted in the kingdom.

Thus the man who served as a pastor but who had a secret sin life will find at the Bema that he will not rule with Christ at all. He had honor and authority in this life which he won't have in the next.

The woman who served as a Bible teacher and discipler of younger women who had a secret sin life will discover the same thing. She will not rule and will not have authority in the life to come.

What you are now is in a sense what you will be forever. So we better pay attention to God's Word now so we can become what we'd like to be forever.

The way in which a believer who has a noble and good heart and who heeds God's Word remains that way is by focusing on Christ and on His soon return and on the Judgment Seat of Christ. Verse 18 is clearly Bema-related. Compare it with Luke 19:26 and the entire parable of the Minas.

Comparing the Parable of the Four Soils with the Parable of the Minas (Luke 8:5-18 & 19:11-27)

When we compare the Parable of the Minas with the Parable of the Sower and the Four Soils, we see that they have much in common:

1. The first soil, the wayside soil (on the path) is equal to those enemies of Jesus in Luke 19:14, 27 (representing unbelieving Israel).
2. The second soil, the rocky soil is equal to the third servant who buries his mina (Luke 19:20-26). The Lord Jesus actually calls him a wicked servant in Luke 19:22.
3. The third soil, the weedy soil, is equal to the second servant who only comes back with five minas (Luke 19:18-19). He is not called a wicked or a good servant. He is not told, "Well done, good servant," like the first servant (Luke 19:17). Compare Luke 19:17 and Luke 19:19. He just hears, "You also be over five cities."
4. The fourth soil, the good soil is equal to the good servant (Luke 19:16-17). This is the one who hears, "Well done, good servant" (Luke 19:17) and who receives authority over ten cities.

Why do I connect these two parables? I do so, not only because the connections are clear, but also because both say, "For whoever has, to him more will be given; and whoever does not have, even what he seems to have will be taken from him" (Luke 8:18; 19:26).

Conclusion

The Parable of the Four Soils is really a warning. The Lord wants everyone to beware. This isn't talking about someone else. This is talking about you and me. We need to be aware of our spiritual growth, of the depth of our roots, of our temptations, of the weeds in our life. And we need to take it all to the Lord, asking Him to give us the insight and the strength and the victory.

To be the good soil we must put our roots down deep. To be the good soil we must not let cares, riches, and pleasures hinder our effectiveness for Christ. The bottom line is, to be the good soil *we must take heed how we hear the Word of God each day!*

If your Christian life is a fruit tree, how is it doing? Is it growing well? Is it bearing much mature fruit? Take heed how you hear the Word of God. The Lord Jesus is coming soon, any day now.

The Differences Between the Two Judgments

In 2012 I was approached by Zondervan to take part in a book called *Four Views on the Role of Works at the Final Judgment.* I accepted and the book was released in July of 2013.

Though there were four views in the book, the other three were just three different ways of saying the same thing. I argued that there is no "final judgment" for Christians. Believers in Christ, according to John 5:24, "shall not come into judgment" concerning their eternal destiny.

Here are some distinctions I made:

	Believers	Unbelievers
Works judged?	Yes	Yes
Reason works judges?	Degrees of rewards	Degrees of torment
Destiny based on works?	No	No
Destiny based on faith?	Yes	Yes
When judged?	Before Millennium	After Millennium
Name of judgment	Judgment Seat of Christ	Great White Throne Judgment
Biblical location?	2 Cor 5:9-11	Rev 20:11-15

I was amazed that the other authors who are leading Evangelicals and who read their Bibles would say that there will be a *final judgment* of our works *in order to determine our eternal destiny.* That was completely foreign to the message not only of Ephesians 2:8-9, but of the entire Bible.

They also spoke of something called *final salvation* which will occur at the Great White Throne Judgment. Yet *final salvation* occurred the moment you or I believed in Christ. There is no such thing as some future judgment at which we will be awarded final salvation.

I believe that such a view of judgment is terribly flawed. It results in a works-salvation mentality. No matter how you explain it, if our ultimate destiny is determined by whether our works tip the scale in our favor, then Ephesians 2:8-9 is a lie, eternal salvation is of works, and people will be able to boast.

Common Misperception: Everyone's Works Will One Day Be Judged by Jesus to Determine Everyone's Eternal Destinies

It is common in Christian books, sermons, and Christian education (Bible colleges and seminaries) to be taught about something called *final judgment*. Many people have heard this expression long before they have come to faith in Christ.

The teaching on final judgment has become so prevalent that even the word *judgment*, by itself, is often understood as referring to a coming day when the Lord will judge all of humanity and determine who will spend eternity with the Lord Jesus and who will be cast into the lake of fire. Recently I heard Dr. Robert Jeffress, Pastor of First Baptist Church of Dallas, say on the radio that anyone who bails out on his ministry or marriage will soon face *God's judgment*. While he surely was talking about the *temporal* judgment of born-again people and not the *eternal condemnation* of unbelievers, it struck me that some might have misunderstood his point. I know that I personally make a habit to speak of *temporal judgment*, rather than merely *judgment*, when I am speaking of God's judgment of believers in this life, for fear that people will misconstrue my words.

Sadly, confusion about judgment can actually keep someone from being born again, or can result in born-again people losing assurance of their eternal destiny.

Speaking of "The Necessity of Obedience [for final salvation] in Galatians," Thomas R. Schreiner says,

Galatians made it clear that these works [Spirit-energized works] are necessary for eternal life. Those don't sow to the Spirit will not experience eternal life. Those who practice the works of the flesh will be excluded from the kingdom.[1]

In this way of thinking, believers must go through life uncertain of their eternal destiny. They must "sow to the Spirit," if they hope to "experience eternal life" and avoid being "excluded from the kingdom."

The renowned American theologian and preacher Jonathan Edwards, in a sermon entitled "The Final Judgment," similarly said:

> If God has appointed a day to judge the world, let us judge and condemn ourselves for our sins. This we must do, if we would not be judged and condemned for them on that day. If we would escape condemnation, we must see that we justly may be condemned. We must be so sensible of our vileness and guilt, as to see that we deserve all that condemnation and punishment which are threatened. And that we are in the hands of God, who is the sovereign disposer of us, and will do with us as seemeth to himself good. Let us therefore often reflect on our sins, confess them before God, condemn and abhor ourselves, be truly humbled, and repent in dust and ashes.[2]

I am reminded of a conversation I had in the summer of 2000 with a five-point Calvinist pastor and seminary professor. Over breakfast I asked him if all those who are born again persevere in faith and good works. He said, "Yes." I then asked, "Doesn't the Bible say that it is impossible to be sure that we will persevere while we are still in this life?" He said, "Of course. If even the Apostle Paul was unsure that he would persevere as he indicated in 1 Cor 9:27, then we certainly can't be sure we will either." I then asked if that meant that we couldn't be sure of our eternal destiny until after we died. His answer was honest and alarming. He said:

---

[1] Robert N. Wilkin, Thomas R. Schreiner, James D. G. Dunn, Michael B. Barber, *Four Views on the Role of Works at the Final Judgment,* ed. Alan P. Stanley (Grand Rapids, MI: Zondervan, 2013), 83.

[2] Jonathan Edwards, "The Final Judgment." See http://www.biblebb.com/files/edwards/final-judgment.htm. Accessed April 29, 2010.

Well, I see in my life what I think are the works of the Spirit. However, I must admit that it is possible that I could fall away. If I did, then I would prove that I was really never born again in the first place, and I would go to hell.

That man is very warm and gracious. I like him. But I am concerned about him because he lives each day in uncertainty. I myself struggled with uncertainty from ages 6 to 20 and was tormented nearly daily by the thought of spending eternity in torment. It is the mistaken doctrine of the final judgment that contributes to this lack of assurance and works-salvation mentality.

In a December 31, 2007 post, Dr. John Piper expresses his confidence as well as his lack of certainty as to how he will fare at *the final judgment*. In his conclusion he is referring to the Great White Throne Judgment of Rev 20:11-15:

Therefore, when I say that what is written in the books is a public confirmation of our faith and of union with Christ, I do not mean that the record will contain more good works than bad works. I mean that there will be recorded there the kind of change that shows the reality of faith—the reality of regeneration and union with Christ. There will be enough evidences of grace that God will be able to make a public display of what is in the books to verify the born-again reality of those written in the book of life. No one is saved on the basis of his works. But everyone who is saved does new works. Not perfectly, but with humble longing for more holiness. That is how I enter 2008, confident that my condemnation is past (Romans 8:3), and that my name is in the book of life, and that the one who began a good work in me will bring it to completion at the day of Christ. I pray for you, that you are with me.[3]

There is a lot of hedging there. How does one know that he has shown "the kind of change that shows the reality of faith—the reality of regeneration and union with Christ?" I recently heard a speaker wonder about a man who slept with over 50 women the year before he came to faith in Christ. That year he only slept with

---

[3]John Piper, "What Will the Final Judgment Mean for You?" See http://www. desiringgod.org/ResourceLibrary/TasteAndSee/ByDate/2007/2550_What_Will_the_ Final_Judgment_Mean_for_You/. Accessed April 29, 2010.

two different women. Does that show that he is born again, or not born again, he asked?

What represents "enough evidences of grace"? What are these "new works" that indicate we are truly born again?

It is true that Piper says he is "confident that [his] condemnation is past [and] that [his] name is in the book of life." However, confidence is not the same as certainty. Within the Reformed thought of Pastor John Piper, confidence means hopefulness. Like the Reformed pastor I spoke with in 2000, he thinks his works are the real deal. But notice that in order for that to be true, his works must be brought to completion. That is, he must persevere.

What Dr. Piper is saying is that if there is insufficient evidence in our works that prove the reality of our faith, then we will go to hell. Indeed the title of the article suggests as much: "What Will the Final Judgment Mean for You?"

But how can anyone have enough works to prove he is regenerate? No one can. Besides, even if someone was extremely confident that he was okay right now, he could not be sure he would not fall in the future. Any one of us can fall. The New Testament is filled with warnings to believers about the danger of falling.

For years I feared a final judgment to determine my eternal destiny. Every day I carried around the fear. Maybe you did as well. If so, we can and should be very sympathetic toward those who still face those struggles. Maybe you are struggling with fear of final judgment even today. If so, you don't need to.

You don't need to worry about final judgment. We are accountable to the Lord Jesus Christ, of course. And everyone, believer and unbeliever, will be judged after this life is over. However, no one will be judged to determine his eternal destiny, as we shall see from Scripture.

How can you be sure of your eternal destiny? The Lord Jesus repeatedly says how you can be sure in the Gospel of John. Let's look at one verse, John 5:24, that summarizes the message Jesus gave over and over again in the Fourth Gospel:

> "Most assuredly, I say to you, He who hears my word and believes in Him who sent me has everlasting life, and shall not come into judgment, but has passed from death into life."

There Is No Judgment of Believers to Determine Their Eternal Destiny (John 5:24)

The statement by the Lord in John 5:24 is one of the most magnificent statements of eternality of the life that Jesus gives to the believer. The Lord uses three different verb tenses—present, future, and past—to make His point. All three tenses are dealing with one point: the one who believes in Jesus has everlasting life that can never be lost.

The future tense statement is that the one who believes in Jesus "shall not come into judgment." In context this means no believer will come into judgment *regarding his eternal destiny.* We do know from many other texts that believers will indeed be judged by Jesus one day to determine their degree of reward in the kingdom (e.g., Matthew 16:27; Luke 19:11-27; Romans 14:10-12; 1 Corinthians 4:1-5; 9:24-27; 2 Corinthians 5:9-10; James 5:9; 1 John 2:28). But here the Lord is speaking of a different judgment, the judgment of eternal condemnation.

The Lord is unequivocally saying that there is no *final judgment of the believer.* Believers will only be judged to determine degree of reward, not to determine where they go. All believers are secure forever, even those who are not watchful (cf. 1 Thessalonians 5:10).[4]

The Judgment of the Works of Believers at the Bema Is to Determine Degree of Reward, Not Eternal Destiny (2 Corinthians 5:1-11)

For years when I preached this passage I only covered 2 Corinthians 5:9-11. I have come to see, however, that verses 1-8 are crucial to set the context. The reason why Paul speaks of believers being judged for "the things done *in the body*" (emphasis added) in verse 10 is

---

[4] It should be noted that Dr. John Piper does comment on John 5:24 in the blog previously cited, saying: "When Jesus says, 'Whoever hears my word and believes him who sent me has eternal life. *He does not come into judgment,* but has passed from death to life,' I take him to mean that we will not be *condemned* in the final judgment, because our sentence has already been passed—not guilty. So why are we there at the last judgment?" He goes on to answer that we are there to show that God's grace indeed transformed our lives. But what must not be missed is that he does not see John 5:24 as teaching that there is no judgment to determine the eternal destiny of believers. Note that even when discussing John 5:24 he speaks of "the final judgment." In his view all will be judged there, and only those whose works prove they are regenerate will escape the lake of fire.

because in verses 1-8 Paul emphasizes the pain and suffering we experience in these decaying bodies as compared with the pain-free glorified bodies we anticipate receiving at the time of the Rapture. Our eternal rewards will be based on what we do in service for Christ in these fallen bodies, not with what we will do in the future in glorified bodies.

It hit me recently, however, that there is another reason why verses 1-8 help explain verses 9-11. Paul makes it clear that we are certain that we will receive these glorified bodies (verses 1-5). There is no doubt of the eternal destiny of his readers, or of any believer.

The Judgment Seat of Christ truth found in verses 9-11 is built on *certainty* of our glorified bodies and hence our certainty of our eternal destiny. In other words, assurance of our eternal destiny underlies Paul's teachings on the Judgment Seat of Christ.

Paul says that "we all," meaning all born-again people, "must appear before the judgment seat of Christ." The reason is "that each one may receive the things done in the body, according to what he has done, whether good or bad."

Tying this in with Paul's remarks in his first epistle to the Corinthians, we know that only those believers who persevere will be approved (*dokimos*). Paul feared disapproval (*adokimos*, 1 Corinthians 9:27). But by the end of his life he could say, "I have fought the good fight, I have finished the race, I have kept the faith" (2 Timothy 4:7). Thus he could joyously say, "Finally, there is laid up for me the crown of righteousness, which the Lord, the righteous Judge, will give to me on that Day [the Bema], and not to me only but also to all who have loved His appearing" (2 Timothy 4:8).

In his second letter to the Thessalonians, Paul urges the believers there to be watchful regarding Christ's soon return, a theme from the Olivet Discourse (cf. Matthew 24:42-44; 25:13). But Paul encourages them that in any case, they will not go through the Tribulation: "For God did not appoint us for wrath [i.e., the Tribulation], but to obtain salvation [i.e., deliverance from the Tribulation via the Rapture] through our Lord Jesus Christ, who died for us, that whether we wake [literally, *whether we watch*] or sleep, we should live together with Him" (1 Thessalonians 5:9-10).

This same teaching is found in many passages (e.g., Matthew 16:24-28; 19:28-30; Luke 19:11-27; 1 Corinthians 4:1-5; Gal 6:7-9; 2

Timothy 2:12; James 5:9; 1 Peter 4:13; 1 John 2:28; 1 John 4:17-19; Revelation 2:26; 3:21).

The Destiny of Unbelievers Is Based on Their Unbelief, Not Their Works (Rev 20:11-15)

It might be accurate to speak of the judgment of unbelievers at the Great White Throne Judgment as their *final judgment*. After all, it is judgment, and it is final.

However, the Bible never specifically calls it *final judgment*,[5] and the basis of condemnation is not the judgment of the works of the unbelievers. The basis of condemnation is not being found in the Book of Life. After the books (plural) containing the works of all people are examined, then a separate book, the Book of Life is opened. Notice what we learn about this book: "And anyone not found written in the Book of Life was cast into the lake of fire" (Revelation 20:15).

Opening the Book of Life to see who is in there is not called a judgment. And it doesn't seem that it is judgment in any normal sense of that term.

Therefore, I would say that it is a bit misleading even for unbelievers to speak of "final judgment" as though that judgment is where their eternal destinies will be decided. Those destinies are already decided. That is simply where their destinies *will be announced.*

Even a casual reading of Revelation 20:11-15 shows that there are two separate issues. The judgment concerns the books, plural, that are opened. These are books containing the works, good and bad, of all people.

While the text does not specifically say the reason for opening the books, we know from other Scripture that everyone will be recompensed according to his works (e.g., Matthew 16:27). That includes unbelievers. Unbelievers will receive degrees of suffering in the lake of fire depending on their works in this life.

Possibly a second reason why the books are opened is to show that no one present is sinless. Someone might claim, absent the books, that he never once sinned. The books will refute such a claim and show that no one present is worthy of entering the kingdom on the basis of his works.

---

[5]Indeed, the expression "final judgment" doesn't occur anywhere in the Bible.

But after the books are opened and examined, a separate book is opened. This is the Book of Life, which reveals who goes to the New Earth and who goes to the lake of fire. Anyone not found written in the Book of Life is cast into the lake of fire.

Hence, the basis of condemnation is found in *the Book* (singular), not in *the books* (plural).

Will there be believers *present* at the Great White Throne Judgment? Quite probably there will be. In the first place, when will Millennial saints be judged? Possibly they will be judged at this occasion to determine their degree of reward for the New Earth.

In the second place, it is likely that OT and Church Age believers will be present *as witnesses*.

In the third place, the fact that the text says "anyone not found written in the book..." suggests that there will be people present who are written in the book.

What about Matthew 7:21-23?

One of the more famous sayings in the Sermon on the Mount is Jesus saying that not all who say, "Lord, Lord," to Him will enter the kingdom, but he who does the will of the Father. This has been used to promote Lordship Salvation, the view that one must not only believe in Jesus to have everlasting life, but must also yield to His Lordship and persevere in that yieldedness to death.

While Matthew 7:21-23 is indeed dealing with the Great White Throne Judgment, it is not teaching Lordship Salvation and it is not teaching that the traditional understanding of *final judgment*. The text makes this clear if we look at it carefully.

The first issue is what the will of the Father is. What did Jesus mean? Was He warning His legalistic Jewish listeners that they had to be better Pharisees and more legalistic to escape eternal condemnation? Hardly. He repeatedly explained to the legalists that the sole condition of eternal life is faith in Him, not works (cf. John 6:28-29).

The will of the Father is to believe in His Son for the promise of everlasting life. This is borne out by the uses of the expression *the will of the Father* in the Gospels. See especially John 6:39-40: "This is the will of the Father who sent Me, that of all He has given Me I should lose nothing, but should raise it up on the last day. And this is the will of Him who sent Me, that everyone who sees the Son and believes in Him may have everlasting life, and I will raise him up on the last day." The will of the Father is that all who believe in the Son have everlasting life now and guaranteed bodily resurrection (with glorified bodies) when the Lord Jesus returns.

The second issue is what is meant by the words, "Have we not prophesied in Your name, cast out demons in Your name, and done many wonders in Your name?" Note the repetition of *in Your name*. These are all good works they claim to have done in Jesus' name.

What they mean is obvious. "That day" refers to the Great White Throne Judgment. On that day many will point to works they did in Jesus' name as proving they should be permitted to enter the kingdom. This claim is unmistakable.

The third issue is what was wrong with what they said. Many assume the problem is that they didn't really do these works. Others assume they did these sorts of works, since even unregenerate people can be priests, pastors, missionaries, and so forth, but that they did not have sufficient good works to prove that they were recipients of grace, as Dr. Piper suggests.

But that is not borne out by Jesus' response in verse 23. Jesus does not deny their claim. His response strongly suggests that their claim is true, but irrelevant, or worse yet, damning.

On what basis do these people argue that Jesus should let them into the kingdom? On the basis of their works. Not on the basis of their faith in Jesus. They do not even mention believing in Him. They only appeal to their works.

The second Kennedy question in Evangelism Explosion is this:

> If you were to die today and God were to ask you why He should let you into His heaven, what would you say? The correct answer is: You should let me in because the Lord Jesus said, "He who believes in Me has everlasting life." I believed in Him for everlasting life, so I have it. And all who have everlasting life enter the kingdom.

The wrong answers all revolve around works: "I try to follow the Golden Rule." "I'm better than most." "My good works outweigh my bad works." "I pray and read my Bible daily and go to church each week."

The answer of verse 22 is the type of answer that anyone trained in Evangelism Explosion would say reveals a works-salvation mindset.

Matthew 7:21-23 *refutes* works salvation.

When Jesus opens the books of deeds at the Great White Throne Judgment, it will be clear who did what and for what reason. But no matter how many good deeds a person did in Jesus' name, if he did not believe in Him for everlasting life, then he will not be found in the Book of Life and Jesus will announce that He never knew the person.

There will likely be no false posturing at this judgment, for the evidence will be clear. Only a fool would claim to have done works in Jesus' name if he did not since the evidence is irrefutable. The problem with these people will not be that they failed to do the works. The problem will be that they failed to do the will of the Father. They failed to believe in His Son.

The fact that they say they did these works *in Jesus' name* strongly suggests that these are unregenerate people *from within Christianity.* These are not Buddhists, Hindus, Muslims, Animists, Atheists, or the like.

Finally, if we compare verses 21-23 with the preceding context, we see that these people are on the broad road of destruction (Matt 7:13-14). After all, the first thing they claim is to have prophesied in Jesus' name. They are representatives of the false prophets of verses 15-20. Those false prophets are known "by their fruits." The fruits there do not speak of their works, for they look good on the outside (they come in sheep's clothing, verse 15). The fruits in question are their words, their teachings (cf. Matthew 12:33-37 where the Lord links trees and their fruit with words spoken). We know false prophets by what they teach about Jesus and particularly about the condition of everlasting life.

Matthew 7:21-23 does not teach that there will be a final judgment of all people, regenerate and unregenerate. Only unregenerate people are mentioned here. And it does not teach that the basis of their condemnation is their works. It teaches just the opposite. The basis of their condemnation is their reliance on their works and their concomitant failure to have believed in Jesus for everlasting life during this life.

So What Difference Does It Make?

Assurance Is at Stake

Unless we know that believers will never be judged to determine where they spend eternity as Jesus promised in John 5:24, we can't be sure we have everlasting life that will never be lost.

What is sweeping Evangelicalism today is the idea that there is a coming final judgment of our works to determine who gets in and who does not. That teaching makes assurance impossible.

Eternal Destiny Is at Stake

As Matthew 7:21-23 shows, if a person believes in works salvation, he is not born again (unless he formerly believed in salvation by grace through faith apart from works).

Anyone who believes in Jesus for everlasting life has that life, shall not come into judgment, and has already passed from death into life. By believing that promise, we know with certainty that we are saved once and for all (once saved, always saved), that we are eternally secure in Jesus.

But if a person thinks he must do good works in order to get into the kingdom, he does not believe that the sole condition is faith in Christ, at least not faith as it is commonly used in the Bible and everyday speech.

Our Ability to Evangelize Clearly Hangs in the Balance

If we believe the "salvation" a person has now is temporary or uncertain and that what ultimately matters is "final salvation," then we will preach that when we evangelize. Instead of "believe on the Lord Jesus Christ and you shall be saved," people will say, "Deny yourself, take up your cross, and follow Christ." Works, not faith, will become the measure of "final salvation."

Assurance Promotes Love, Gratitude, and a Robust Christian Life

Does assurance of final destiny apart from works move us to rebellion? Does the promise of eternal security promote lawlessness and wickedness? No way. While it is certainly *possible* to abuse grace, one can only do so by neglecting the powerful motivation of gratitude that eternal security provides. And to walk in the darkness requires one to live contrary to the knowledge that one day we will appear at the Judgment Seat of Christ and have our works evaluated and recompensed. Do we not long to hear our Lord, Savior, and Judge say, "Well done, good servant" (Luke 19:17)?

In addition, if a believer foolishly rebels against God, he will reap *temporal* judgment. The prodigal son (Luke 15:11-32) found poverty, famine, and pain when he left the fellowship of his father (Luke 15:14). "No one gave him anything," we are told (Luke 15:16). The son came to his senses and returned to his father, not because his eternal destiny was at stake, but because his temporal well-being hung in the balance.

A failure to distinguish between temporal judgment and eternal condemnation is a terrible error. It is one that can actually keep people away from faith in Christ because as long as a person thinks he must persevere in good works in order to succeed in "the final judgment," he does not believe the promise of John 5:24.

When I was a senior in college I came to believe in Jesus for everlasting life and thus to know I was secure forever. This knowledge transformed me. I changed from pre-Med to pre-Ministry. I devoted the rest of my life to telling others this wonderful news.

Having grown up in an alcoholic family and having struggled with perfectionism all my life, I'm not confident that my works will prove to myself, others, or the Lord Jesus, that I've received the grace of God. While I'm not what I used to be, I'm also not what I'm going to be (1 John 3:2). I'd be scared to death if I thought I would one day face some final judgment of my works to see if I'm going to the lake of fire. This isn't because I have some secret life of immorality or drunkenness. It is because I fall short of the glory of God all the time (Romans 3:23) and because of the fact that I have lots of flaws in my thinking, speaking, and acting.

Dr. R. C. Sproul in a 1989 article indicated he is not sure of his eternal destiny, but that "being uncomfortable with Jesus is better than any other option." He is not alone. All who believe in a future final judgment for believers think that way.

Since they can't be sure whether they will persevere in faith and good works or not, then they naturally fear the so-called *final judgment*—something that believers will not even face. "Being uncomfortable with Jesus" is thus probably the best option for someone, Calvinist or Arminian, who believes that he must persevere in faith and good works till death in order to escape eternal condemnation.

By keeping busy, one can hopefully keep these "moments of acute self-awareness" to a minimum. But one will always carry around fear of hell if he believes that he will not discover his eternal destiny *until the final judgment.*

As the Lord said in John 5:24, the one who simply believes in Him *has* (present tense) everlasting life. That is, he has life that can never be lost! That is good news.

And the one who simply believes in Him has already, past tense, passed from death into life. That is good news.

Indeed, the one who simply believes in Him shall not, future tense in the negative, come into judgment concerning his eternal destiny. That too is good news.

You don't need to worry about final judgment since there is no final judgment to determine the eternal destiny of believers. And you won't worry about a so-called final judgment as long as you remember the promise of the Lord Jesus Christ that the one who believes in Him shall not come into judgment.

Conclusion

The issue in eschatological judgment of believers and unbelievers is recompense for work done (rewards or degree of torment), not life.

Believers are judged before the Millennium to determine degrees of reward in the kingdom. Unbelievers are judged after the Millennium to determine degrees of torment in the lake of fire.

No believer or unbeliever will be judged to determine his eternal destiny. That is set at the moment of faith (believers) or death (unbelievers).

Every believer will be judged to determine his eternal rewards. Some will be weighed and found wanting. May that not be true of us. We should long for His praise and approval.

Grace and the Bema: Why We'll Get More than We Deserve

Introduction

Athletics play a big part of the American psyche. We love our high school, college, and pro sports teams. Most Americans have some sport as a hobby: running, golf, fishing, hunting, tennis, volleyball, basketball, softball are just a few examples.

Christians Are Like Athletes Competing for Prizes

The Bible uses lots of athletic metaphors related to the Christian life. The Apostle Paul compared the Christian life to running a race or fighting a fight. The author of Hebrews also spoke of the race that is set before us. The Lord Jesus in the Book of Revelation calls Christians to be overcomers. The Greek word translated *overcomers* is *nikaō*. The noun form is *nikē*, the Greek word for victor or winner. We are all called to be overcoming, victorious Christians, Nike Christians.

There is a major difference between being on God's team and being on a secular sports teams. The difference is grace. There is lots of grace extended to our running of the Christian race.

Getting on the Team and Staying on the
Team Is by Grace, Not Works

As I've mentioned numerous times, all who simply believe in Jesus
have eternal life. That is, every one who merely believes in Him is
eternally secure, no strings attached.

Jesus said, "He who believes in Me has everlasting life" (John
6:47). It really is that simple. Just believe in Him and you are eternally secure.

Well, now that you have eternal life, what are you going to do
with it? You may have 50 or 60 or more years left in this life before
you are raptured or die. Will you use your eternal life wisely? And
what will motivate you to do so, since you are eternally secure?

The Bema Should Motivate All Christians
to Be Victors/Overcomers

It is my contention that the Judgment Seat of Christ, also called the
Bema, is a powerful motivation to live for God now. And when we
think of all the grace of God associated with our judgment at the
Bema, the motivation goes up even more.

Let's begin by considering what the Bema is and is not.

What the Bema Is and Is Not

The Bema Is the Time When Believers Will Be Judged
to Determine Their Position in Jesus' Kingdom

Second Corinthians 5:9-10 says,

> Therefore we make it our aim, whether present or absent,
> to be well pleasing to Him. For we all must appear before
> the judgment seat of Christ, that each one may receive the
> things *done* in the body, according to what he has done,
> whether good or bad.

The Bema is the time after the Rapture when all Christians will
be judged for the works they did in life, both good and bad. The
Lord Jesus will there announce what each Christians has earned in
terms of eternal rewards.

These rewards will include undefined treasure (Matthew 6:19-21),
degrees of rulership with Christ (Luke 19:11-27; 2 Timothy 2:12),

degrees of abundance of life (John 10:10; Gal 6:8), and special privileges and honors (Revelation 2-3, 22).

The Bema is not merely a time of rejoicing and receiving of praise and rewards. according to the Apostle John, the experience of some Christians will be primarily one of shame (1 John 2:28). Some Christians won't hear the Lord's commendation: "Well done, good servant" (Luke 19:17). Some won't rule at all with Christ (Luke 19:20-26).

The Bema should not be thought of like a children's soccer tournament, where 100% of the contestants get prizes and praise and hugs.

James reminds us that "the Judge is at the door" (James 5:9). We need to realize that Jesus is not only our Savior and Lord, He is also our Judge.

The Bema Is Not the Believer's "Final Judgment" and It Is Not the Great White Throne Judgment

Many Christians envision one final judgment of all people, believers and unbelievers, to determine each person's eternal destiny.

This way of thinking stems from the idea that no one can be sure of his or her eternal destiny until after he dies and appears at the final judgment.

Arminians believe that one can lose eternal life by failure to persevere.

Some Calvinists believe you can prove you never had eternal life in the first place by failure to persevere.

Yet in John 5:24 Jesus promises that the one who believes in Him "shall not come into judgment/condemnation."

And in John 3:18 the Lord said the one who believes in Him is not condemned. That is, the believer is in a state of non-condemnation and he will never experience condemnation. If you don't realize this, you will fall into thinking that we must do good works in order to get into the kingdom.

Grace is God's favor and it is unearned and unmerited. Romans 4:4-5 makes this point clearly:

> Now to him who works, the wages are not counted as grace but as debt. But to him who does not work but believes on Him who justifies the ungodly, his faith is counted as righteousness.

We lose our grip on grace if we aren't absolutely sure we have eternal life simply by virtue of our faith in Christ, apart from any works now or in the future.

Thus the number-one aspect of grace at the Bema is that we are justified by faith apart from works. To qualify for the Bema one must merely be born again. No strings attached. All believers are eternally secure. That is grace and that is good news.

Actually there are two separate eschatological judgments in Scripture: the Great White Throne Judgment for unbelievers (Revelation 20:11-15) and the Judgment Seat of Christ, the Bema, for believers (2 Corinthians 5:9-10). The Bema occurs before the Millennium. The Great White Throne Judgment occurs after the Millennium.

Many Christians mistakenly think that these are two different names for the same judgment and that both will occur at the end of the eschaton. Not so. They are different judgments occurring at different times for different groups of people and for different purposes.

The purpose of the Bema is to announce each believer's position and privileges in the life to come, his or her degree of abundance of all. All will have joyful lives. All will glorify Christ. But some will be much more joyful because some will have much more capacity and opportunity to glorify Christ.

The purpose of the Great White Throne Judgment is to give each unbeliever their day in court, to prove they are condemned because they were neither sinless nor did they believe in Jesus, and to announce each unbelievers' degree of torment in the lake of fire. Their works are evaluated both to show they have no claim on God, and to determine their degree of punishment forever.

Staying in Contention to Win the Prize Is a Matter of Grace

Let's compare the Christian competition with secular competition.

Secular competition	Christian competition	Scripture
Few actually make team	All believers are on team	2 Corinthians 5:10
Only the best win	All who persevere win	2 Timothy 2:12
All or nothing on winning	Degrees of winning	Luke 19:17, 19
Little care for you	Intense love for you	1 John 4:19
No inner help	Holy Spirit enables	Romans 8:8-11
Prizes are perishable	Prizes are imperishable	1 Corinthians 9:25
The coach's approval fades	Jesus' approval is eternal	1 Corinthians 9:27

There Will Be Lots of Grace at the Bema

We Will Be Judged by What We Did with the Time We Had (Matthew 25:14-30)

We will not be judged based on a comparison of how we did in relation to someone else. To whom much is given, much is required. The more God gives you, the more that is expected of you. The Parable of the Talents shows that one who maximizes his or her life with less ability can and will receive as much as the one who maximizes his or her abilities with more abilities.

We Will Be Judged by What We Did with the Time We Had (Matthew 20:1-16)

The Parable of the Day Laborers in Matthew 20:1-16 is often misunderstood to be saying that all believers will have the same reward in the kingdom. That can't be because it is clear from the Parable of the Minas that there will be distinctions.

This parable teaches that we won't be penalized if we have less time to work due to circumstances outside our control. Most likely the Lord has the Rapture in mind. Some believers will be in Bible College or Seminary when the Rapture occurs. No one will be penalized for what they didn't do as a result of the rapture. The same would apply to those who die prematurely as long as their death was not a result of God's judgment in their lives due to sin.

There is much grace in this. Just do the best with the time you have and don't worry about the time you don't have.

We Store Up Mercy When We Are Merciful (James 2:13)

Judgment at the Bema will be merciless to the one has shown no mercy. So if you want mercy at the Bema, be merciful yourself.

There is grace in this too. As in video games when you gain bonus time for doing something good, so in this life when we are merciful to others we gain a special measure of mercy for ourselves at the Bema. God didn't have to do it that way. He could have simply judged us all straight up. But He not only will reward us for the acts of mercy we do, but He will also multiply that act by giving us more mercy in our judgment.

We Will Receive Bonuses for Wholehearted Service (Luke 19:17, 19)

If we were setting up a system of eternal rewards, we'd surely say that only those who wholeheartedly serve God throughout their lives will get any rewards. But God gives rewards for all who persevere, even those who are less than wholehearted.

Compare Luke 19:17 and Luke 19:19. Note the difference in what each is told. Both are rewarded. Both will rule in the life to come.

But only the wholehearted servant is praised. Only he hears, "Well done, good servant."

The wholehearted servant gets authority over twice as many cities too, ten instead of five.

Application: Knowing About God's Grace and the Bema Should Have a Profound Impact on Our Lives

It Produces an Enormous Amount of Gratitude (2 Corinthians 5:14)

We should be grateful for the gift of eternal life and the knowledge that we are eternally secure by faith in Jesus. We should also be grateful that He chooses to reward us for what we do for Him.

What a deal. He gives us everything and then not only rewards us, but is very gracious in His evaluation of our lives.

It Moves Us to Be Merciful to Others (James 2:13)

Knowing the degree of mercy we receive at the Bema will be related to the mercy we showed in this life should wake us all up to be merciful to others.

Here is a painful personal example. I hired a friend to be my secretary in a very small office. She wasn't working out. I was very new to being an employer. Her 3-month probationary time was expiring just after Thanksgiving. She and her husband had my wife and me over for Thanksgiving. A few days later I let her go. While I gave her a little severance pay, I really blew it. I should have let her continue to work for me until she found another job. Live and learn. I won't be getting much mercy at the Bema for that one.

Here is a positive personal example. I hired a guy to work for me who had a seminary degree and who had just earned an MBA. He had good references. But when he came to work for me, he wasn't very productive. He liked to have meetings and talk. But he didn't get much done in our small office. After about eight months, I told him that this wasn't going to work, that this wasn't a good fit for his skills and the needs we had. I gave him up to four months to find another job. He left on good terms and I felt I had learned. Maybe I stored up some mercy at the Bema.

It Motivates Us to Be Humble (1 Corinthians 4:7)

What do we have that we did not receive from God? (1 Corinthians 4:7). God resists the proud but gives grace to the humble (James 4:6).

It Answers the Question, "Why Not Live Like the Devil?"

There are many reasons why we shouldn't live like the devil: gratitude, desire for God's blessings now, desire to avoid His hand of discipline now, but also a recognition that the quality of my eternal experience hangs in the balance on how I live.

The Bema is a powerful reason to live for God.

*It Causes Us to Keep Our Focus on the Bema and
on Christ's Approval (1 Corinthians 9:24-27).*

Clearly Paul was focused on the Bema. He indicates this in
1 Corinthians 9:24-27. Then, at the end of his life, shortly before he
was martyred he could write, "I have fought the good fight. I have
finished the course. I have kept the faith" (2 Timothy 4:8).

The Lord Jesus commanded us to lay up treasure in heaven and to
set our heart on heavenly treasure (Matthew 6:19-21).

Clearly while Christians should experience abundant lives now,
our ultimate aim should be fixed on the Bema.

Conclusion

I received the Obsessive-Compulsive award at Dallas Theological
Seminary all seven years I was a student there. Well, not really, since
there was no such award (unless the Ph.D. degree is that award).
But I am a lot like the character Monk on the TV show (or Bob in
the movie *What About Bob?*).

It is easy for me to obsess on things, especially something like a
one-time judgment in which the quality of my entire eternal experience will be determined. Yet I find I am not paralyzed when I
think about the Bema. Why?

I believe it is because I know God loves me and wants me to succeed. I know He is gracious. I know there is a lot of grace in the
Christian life and there will be a lot of grace extended at the Bema.

Obviously those who aren't sure they have eternal life aren't concerned about eternal rewards. Their concern is where they go when
they die.

Those of us who are certain we have eternal life simply by faith in
Jesus are free to focus on the Bema and potential fullness of life in
the life to come.

I long to hear the Lord say, "Well done, good servant." My appreciation for His grace makes that so important to me. My focus on
the Bema leaves me highly motivated to invest my life in things that
count. Live each day in light of the Bema. You'll be forever glad you
did.

Section 6
Study Guide

"Study to show yourself approved unto God, a workman that needs not to be ashamed, rightly dividing the word of truth."

2 Timothy 2:15 (KJV 2000)

Why Study?

Bible study is a great way to grow in our faith. The questions in this Study Guide may be used for personal or group study. They are designed to make you think. The chapters provide the background to help you discover the answers.

If you discuss these questions in a group setting, you will surely find differences of opinion. Let those differences move you to look carefully at the Word of God, where the answers are to be found.

May we all be like the Bereans who searched the Scriptures daily to see if the things spoken by Paul and Silas were true (Acts 17:11).

STUDY 1

The Disaster of Poor Communication

1. Give an example of a time when you were the victim of poor communication. What was the result?

2. Is there any price an unbeliever must pay in order to gain eternal life? Please explain and defend your answer biblically.

3. How does distinguishing eternal life from eternal rewards affect your understanding of assurance?

4. How is this distinction important for a clear communication of the gospel?

5. How does being properly motivated in your Christian service depend on understanding the difference between eternal life and eternal rewards?

6. As a Christian, have you ever lacked assurance (the certain knowledge that because of faith in Jesus you have eternal life and could never lose it)? If so, how did you regain it? If not, what has helped you stay sure you are eternally secure?

7. If you doubt that you are secure based on God's promise alone, your object of assurance becomes yourself instead of Christ. How would this affect your relationship with Him?

8. What happens to your understanding of the rewards passages of the New Testament when you lose sight of the fact that the only thing God requires of you for eternal life is faith in His immutable promise?

STUDY 2

Wages Aren't Gifts

1. Does the term *gift* have multiple meanings?

2. If eternal rewards are pay for work done, doesn't this cheapen the death of Christ on your behalf? Defend your answer.

3. If you don't distinguish between earned rewards and the gift of eternal life, what are the potential practical difficulties in your life?

4. Why do you think some pastors and theologians argue that all believers will have the same quality of life in the kingdom and that rewards are gifts, not payments for work performed?

5. Which single verse or passage in the Bible stands out to you as a strong defense for rewards (*misthos*) being compensation for work done? Why?

6. How does the possibility of the Lord rewarding you for your life of service make you feel? Does it encourage you? Motivate you? Or does it discourage you? Why does it make you feel this way?

7. How does knowing that eternal life is free change encourage and motivate the Body of Christ, and change the way you view the doctrine of eternal rewards?

8. Paul wrote Second Timothy just before his execution; thus, it is a very personal view of his heart. Read 2 Timothy 4:6-8. How did Paul understand and respond to the motivation of eternal rewards? What does this mean to you?

STUDY 3

We Really Do Reap What We Sow (Galatians 6:6-10)

1. Why is the principle of sowing and reaping hard for some to believe?

2. Discuss how the analogy of sowing and reaping ties in with the point Paul is making in Galatians 6:6-10.

3. Compare verses 6 and 10. How are they similar and how are they different?

4. In light of Galatians 5, what specifically is sowing to the flesh? Is it, for example, willful rebellion against God as in the case of the Prodigal Son in Luke 15? Defend your answer.

5. Again, in light of Galatians 5, what specifically is meant by sowing to the Spirit?

6. Explain the difference between *possessing* eternal life and *reaping* eternal life.

7. How can eternal life be a free gift received by faith alone (John 4:10; 5:24; 6:47) and also be wages earned for work done (Galatians 6:7-9)? Why isn't this a contradiction?

8. How do you avoid losing heart in your Christian life?

STUDY 4

Faithful Servants (Luke 19:11-27)

1. Compare Luke 19:17 and 19:19. Discuss the similarities and differences between the Lord's response to each servant.

2. Defend the view that the third servant represents an unbeliever.

3. Defend the view that the third servant represents a third type of believer.

4. Who are the enemies of Jesus in this parable and what does their slaying in verse 27 signify?

5. How is Luke 19:11-27 similar to and different from Matthew 25:14-30?

6. Explain Luke 19:21-22. Does God really reap what He didn't sow? What is going on here?

7. What does putting money in the bank illustrate (Luke 19:23)? How could you do that today in a spiritual sense?

8. What does this passage have to say about those who persevere less than wholeheartedly in their service for Christ?

STUDY 5

Loving Disciples (1 John 2:28; 4:17-19)

1. Fear often has an object. You may fear stock market decline, loss of job or health, accidents, terrorist attacks, failure, etc. What is the specific object of fear in 1 John 4:17-19?

2. Are you afraid of "the day of judgment" (1 John 4:17)? Why or why not?

3. What precisely is "perfect love"?

4. Describe a time in your life when you felt confident (had boldness) and one in which you experienced shame. Compare those experiences to 1 John 2:28.

5. If your parents often mistreated you and were unfair with you, how might this affect the way you think about the Bema? If a person has an unhealthy attitude toward the Bema, how might he or she correct that attitude?

6. Give three or more examples in which someone you know showed "perfect love" toward you. How do you think their lives were enhanced by helping you?

7. Do you often reflect on the return of Christ? Do you think it is good to do? Why or why not?

8. What does it mean to "live today in light of eternity"?

STUDY 6

Nike Christians (2 Timothy 2:11-13)

1. What does Paul mean when he speaks of a believer dying with Christ? In what sense have Christians died with Him?

2. Why does Paul speak of living with Christ as future ("we shall also live with Him")? Don't believers already live with Christ?

3. In 2 Timothy 2:12a, what is entailed in the concept of endurance?

4. What does "denying Him" mean (2:12b)? Is this a one-time act, something that characterizes one's life, or how one is when his life ends (in death or the Rapture)? Can a born again person deny Christ in this sense?

5. What does Paul mean when he speaks of the Lord Jesus denying those who deny Him?

6. Explain 2 Timothy 2:13.

7. Explain how you think the following three people will fare at the Bema. (Hint: compare these people to 2 Timothy 2:11-13 and Luke 8:11-15 and Luke 19:11-26.)

    a) Joe served Christ faithfully for thirty years and then drifted away from the Lord. He stopped going to church and no longer confessed His faith in Christ. For the last five years of his life he lives as a secret disciple.

    b) Mary came to faith and began to grow spiritually. But within a year, she drifted away from the Lord. She lived the next forty years of her life as though God didn't exist.

Then after the death of her husband, she returned to fellowship with the Lord. For the last decade of her life she was a growing disciple who openly confessed Christ.

c) Sean came to faith and served Christ halfheartedly his whole adult life. He failed to realize his potential as a Christian. Yet he endured in fellowship with Christ and in confessing Him.

8. Explain Matthew 10:32-33 in light of 2 Timothy 2:11-13.

STUDY 7

Cross Bearers (Matthew 16:24-28)

1. List the four uses of the Greek word *psychē* in Matthew 16:24-28.

2. What does losing one's *psychē* refer to in this context?

3. What does gaining one's *psychē* refer to in this context?

4. How was it possible for the disciples to have eternal life prior to the cross?

5. The Greek word *psychē* is used to speak of the Lord Jesus laying down His *life* for us (Matthew 20:28; Mark 10:45; John 10:11, 15, 17). Compare 1 John 3:16-18 and discuss how His laying down His *psychē* should impact your life.

6. What event preceded the Lord's comments in Matthew 16:24-28? How does keeping the context in mind help you understand these verses?

7. If you could gain the entire world, in terms of money, power, and fame, but you had to forfeit treasure, power, and fame in the life to come, would you do it? Would you be tempted to do it? Why or why not?

8. Does "each" in verse 27 refer to each *believer*? Or does it refer to each and every *person* who has ever lived, including all unbelievers? Defend your answer.

STUDY 8

Humble Followers (Luke 17:7-10)

1. How does Luke 17:5-6 serve as a transition between verses 1-4 and 7-10?

2. In verse 9, does the Lord mean that He will not thank us for our service? Why or why not?

3. What should your attitude be when you work hard and accomplish something while serving the Lord (verse 10)?

4. How does verse 10 apply to the Christian who is not working hard and serving the Lord?

5. Tell about a time that you observed another Christian exemplify a servant's heart. How did this impact you?

6. Compare Luke 17:7-10 with Matthew 23:11 and John 13:4-11.

7. Do you feel a sense of duty in your service for Christ? Why or why not? How can you cultivate a greater sense of duty?

8. Since God has chosen to obligate Himself to reward believers for their service, might there be a danger that we lose a sense of gratitude and develop an entitlement mentality? How can we avoid having such an attitude?

STUDY 9

Heavenly Treasure (Matthew 6:19-21)

1. Write a brief account of someone you know who made significant personal sacrifice in the service of Christ.

2. Is saving for retirement an example of laying up treasure on earth? How about saving enough money for a down payment on a house? Owning a new car? How do you decide when you cross the line from prudent use of the money God has given you to laying up treasure on earth?

3. What does it mean to lay up treasures in heaven? Give concrete examples of how you can do that.

4. Using Revelation 21:24, build a case for the existence of an economy in the eternal kingdom.

5. In what way is heavenly treasure different from treasure on earth?

6. Where will treasure in heaven be enjoyed? Be careful, this is a trick question!

7. What does the Lord mean when He says, "Where your treasure is, there your heart will be also"?

8. In what way is heavenly treasure different from all other eternal rewards?

STUDY 10

Ruling with Christ

1. What are *active* and *passive* inheritances, and what is the biblical justification for these concepts?

2. Name ten different types of rulers in the nation of Israel. You might skim through 1–2 Samuel, 1–2 Kings, or 1–2 Chronicles for ideas.

3. Why would it be desirable to rule with Christ? After all, doesn't rulership entail a lot of hassles?

4. Do you want to rule with Christ? Why or why not?

5. Do you think that there would be a sense of regret for those believers who do not rule with Christ? Why or why not?

6. Consider the halfhearted Christian who will rule with Christ, but with only half the influence he could have had (Luke 19:19, compared with 19:17). Do you think that such a person will have a sense of regret?

7. The twelve disciples wanted to rule with Christ. Was that desires a good or a bad thing? Defend your answer.

8. Does the concept of being one of Christ's *partners* (*metachoi*) in the life to come evoke different feelings in you than the anticipation of being a *co-ruler* with Him? Why or why not?

STUDY 11

Special Privileges

1. Do you think the prospect of earning special privileges is a proper way to motivate people to do their best? Why or why not?

2. Name the three most significant special privileges you ever earned in your family, school, work, or in other areas of life.

3. Why would entering the New Jerusalem by its gates be a privilege worth having?

4. What is the biblical significance of having a stone engraved with some special name that the Lord Jesus has given you?

5. Why would special foods like manna and the fruits of the tree of life be something worth having?

6. Do you find that the prospect of wearing special garments motivates you to serve Christ? Why or why not?

7. How does gaining these special privileges relate to the abundance of life referred to in John 10:10?

8. Explain the significance of ordinary things, such as your name, food, and clothing, being transformed into extraordinary privileges in the life to come. How does this highlight God's love for you?

STUDY 12

His Approval

1. What is approval?

2. What is the difference between approval and acceptance? How does the distinction help you to understand eternal rewards?

3. What was your initial reaction to the idea that the Lord Jesus will not approve of every believer when He judges us at the Bema?

4. What does gaining the approval of the Lord Jesus mean to you? How should it impact your daily living?

5. Will believers experience varying degrees of approval? What does this mean to you practically? Does this motivate you?

6. If a person walks with Christ faithfully for fifty years, then falls away, ceasing to go to church, pray, read the Bible, and confess Him, would he be approved due to his fifty years of service, or disapproved because of ending his life away from the Lord? Does the Bible speak on this? What does it say?

7. Do you think that the concept of approval as an eternal reward, distinct from eternal salvation, might be a helpful one to share with unbelievers? Why or why not?

8. How does the nature of this reward (His approval) help you to realize that, even in rewards, Christ is the focus, instead of yourself or the reward itself? Does this make you appreciate Him more?

STUDY 13

Fullness Forever

1. Does Revelation 4:9-10 teach that you will give back whatever rewards you receive at the Bema? Defend your answer from this passage and from other New Testament verses.

2. Do you agree or disagree that the Millennium is the first 1,000 years of the eternal kingdom?

3. Do you agree or disagree that all eternal rewards last for one thousand years only? Defend your answer.

4. Would it motivate you more to strive for rewards if you knew they lasted forever and not simply for 1,000 years? Why or why not?

5. Pick out a few verses in Revelation 21–22 which suggest that some will rule with Christ in the eternal kingdom.

6. Do you agree or disagree with the suggestion that Matthew 6:19-21 shows that treasure stored in heaven will be everlasting? Why?

7. Do you see any comparisons and/or contrasts between working for many years for a nice retirement and working for Christ for many years so you can have a nice eternity? List some similarities and differences.

8. How does the eternal nature of these rewards magnify the Rewarder and humble the servant?

STUDY 14

Prepare to Meet the Judge (James 5:9)

1. Do you normally think of the Lord Jesus as your Judge? How should His office of Judge affect your perception of Him and your service toward Him?

2. James was probably written within a year of the resurrection, yet believers in the church were already becoming weary of waiting for Christ's return. What does that say about our need to stay focused on Christ's impending return?

3. Compare James 5:9 with Revelation 3:20.

4. In light of James 5:9 and 1 John 1:9, will sins you confess still be judged at the Bema? Why or why not?

5. Does judgment according to works contradict justification by faith alone? Why or why not?

6. John 5:24 says that believers will not come into judgment. Harmonize that passage with James 5:9.

7. What is the door that is referred to in James 5:9? How does this highlight the expectancy of His coming? What does this mean for your relationship with Him?

8. Should you be concerned with His office as Judge, even though He is merciful? How does the Bible express the idea of His coming judgment of believers? Are you really held to a standard?

STUDY 15

Remember Your Inheritance (Galatians 5:19-21)

1. Have you ever inherited anything in which the amount you received reflected your treatment of the deceased? Or, do you know someone who had that experience? Explain what happened.

2. How do you know that Paul isn't saying that good works are required to keep eternal life?

3. Is Paul teaching that those whose lives are characterized by the deeds of flesh are not true believers?

4. Compare Ephesians 2:8-9 with Galatians 5:19-21, paying special attention to the verb tenses.

5. How is 2 Timothy 2:12 related to Galatians 5:19-21?

6. Explain the concepts of being an "heir of God" and a "joint heir with Christ" as found in Romans 8:17. How does this impact you?

7. Look over the list of sins in Galatians 5:19-21. Note some that don't seem to be as bad as others. Why do you think Paul includes seemingly lesser sins in this list?

8. What do the words "those who practice such things" in Galatians 5:21 mean? Is Paul thinking of what characterizes one's life? Of willful rebellion, unconfessed sins, or what?

STUDY 16

Walk Without Stumbling (Jude 24)

1. Do a brief concordance study of Demas. Who was he and what happened to him?

2. Compare Jude 24 with 1 Corinthians 9:24-27.

3. Discuss the New Testament concept of being faultless. Is being faultless synonymous with being a believer? What are the implications of this?

4. What must a Christian do in order for God to keep him from stumbling?

5. When someone categorizes passages like Jude 24 as unconditional promises, what kind of attitude does this create?

6. On the other hand, what kind of attitude comes from knowing that God "is able to keep you from stumbling" if you trust Him to do so?

7. How does this apply to the Christian who has fallen?

8. What does it mean to be "before the presence of His glory with exceeding joy"?

STUDY 17

Keep Your Eyes on the Prize
(1 Corinthians 9:24-27)

1. In what ways is the Christian life like a race?

2. What do crowns signify? Do you think Paul is thinking of literal crowns, literal crowns plus something else, or merely what the crowns symbolize? Defend your answer.

3. Contrast an *imperishable* crown with a *perishable* one.

4. How can you run with certainty in your Christian life?

5. Why does a Christian need to discipline his body?

6. How can a Christian discipline his body?

7. Discuss the New Testament concept of approval (*dokimos*).

8. How does the story of Alfred Rascon relate to your life? When you feel like you've been shot twice, blown up by a grenade, and shot again, are you going to fight on? Are you going to act in self-sacrificing love as he did? How will knowing that the Lord will reward you abundantly with an "imperishable crown" help you to do this?

Subject Index

A

Abide, 35, 37, 83

Abiding, 38–39

Abraham, 52, 106

Abundant Life, 19, 23–25, 78

Acceptance, 82

Adokimos, 16, 82, 113, 153

Ambition, 69, 100

Approval, 16, 34, 81–84, 98, 102, 112, 116–117, 168

Approved, 82–84, 115, 153

Arminian, 113, 163

Assurance, 17, 38, 105, 106, 112, 114, 148, 158–159

Augustine, 126

Authority, 30–31, 34, 69–70, 72–74, 78, 125

B

Baptism, 33

Believe, 17, 20–22, 36–37, 42–43, 96, 107, 114, 117, 138

Believer, 16, 17, 19–21, 21–25, 30, 31–36, 37–39, 42–47, 69, 70–72, 74, 85–89, 116, 141–142

Believers, 96–99, 105–110, 112

Bema, 16, 21, 35–38, 39, 86, 89, 97–98, 143–144, 152, 161–168

Blamelessness, 16

Bold, 16, 36–38

C

Calvinist, 113, 163

Certainty, 22, 93, 112, 151

Co-heir, 70–71, 74

Commitment, 42

Confess, 16, 32–33, 44, 71, 95

Confidence, 35–37, 39–40, 151

Contentment, 20, 126

Costliness, 42

Cross, 36, 42, 49–52, 54

Crown, 86–87, 88, 112, 115–116

D

Day of Judgment, 37–39

Deny, 42–45, 49–50, 53–54

Dillow, 23, 32, 71–72, 89

Disapproval, 16, 153

Disapproved, 82

Discipline, 36, 38, 59, 71, 82, 93, 112

Disqualified, 82, 93, 112

Dokimos, 16, 82, 153

E

Endurance, 43, 45, 98

Entering (the Kingdom), 16, 101, 113, 137

Eternal Life
   duration, 24, 108, 117

Scripture Index

Made in the USA
Charleston, SC
06 April 2014